SIMPLE SCRAPBOOKS

25 Fun & Meaningful
Memory **Books You Can**
Make in a **Weekend**

S t a c y   J u l i a n

with Gayle Humpherys

Introduction by
Lisa Bearnson

CREATING KEEPSAKES BOOKS
Bluffdale, Utah

Published in 2000 by Creating Keepsakes Books, a division of Porch Swing Publishing, Inc., 14901 South Heritage Crest, Bluffdale, UT 84065.
Visit us at www.creatingkeepsakes.com

Printed in U.S.A.

Library of Congress Cataloging-in-Publication data

Julian, Stacy.
    Simple scrapbooks : 25 fun & meaningful memory books you can make in
    a weekend / Stacy Julian with Gayle Humpherys ; introduction by Lisa Bearnson.
        p. cm.
    Includes index.
    ISBN 1-929180-23-3 (hc. : alk. paper) -- ISBN 1-929180-24-1 (pbk. : alk.paper)
    1. Photograph albums. 2. Photographs--Conservation and restoration.
    3. Scrapbooks. I. Humpherys, Gayle. II. Title.
    TR465 .J85 2000
    745.593--dc21

                    00-050825

Creating Keepsakes Books may be purchased in bulk for sales promotions, premiums, or fundraisers. For information, please write to: Special Markets Department, Creating Keepsakes Books, 14901 South Heritage Crest, Bluffdale, UT 84065.

Creating Keepsakes Books
Editorial Office, Washington, D.C.
Director: Maureen Graney
Editor: Stephanie Henke
Index: Sandi Frank

Creating Keepsakes™ magazine
Main Office, Bluffdale, Utah
Creative Director: Don Lambson
Designer: Kate Johnson
Principal Photography: Brian Tweed
Designer: Brian Tippetts
Cofounder: Lisa Bearnson
Cofounder: Don Lambson
Publisher and CEO: Mark Seastrand

Creating Keepsakes™ magazine is published ten times a year. To subscribe, call 888/247-5282

"The Gangs
All Here"

I love these
photos of the
kids goofing
off with each
other. I look at
them and just
count my many
blessings of all
the joy and
laughter they
have brought
into my life.
October 1999

Contents

90

82

59

Ask me to supply one word about Stacy Julian and her scrapbooking style and I'd say, "Inspiring." As the ideas for *Simple Scrapbooks* took form, I was able to sit down with Stacy on several occasions and get a sneak preview of her projects. I found them incredibly touching.

Idea after idea struck an emotional chord—ideas that made me reminisce about my past, cry and want to start scrapbooking immediately. Best of all, I didn't feel overwhelmed. Any of the projects could be completed (yes, I said "completed") in a single weekend. How's that for a switch?

This book is for you and anyone else who wants to create a meaningful album in days, not months or years. Getting started is easy. Just pick one of the 25 fun projects in this book and put someone else in charge of your household this weekend. Gather all the pictures and supplies you need, then hole up in a room where you can work without interruption. You'll love the sense of accomplishment as you emerge with a complete and captivating theme album. Not only will you feel good, your family will love the results as well!

Lisa Bearnson

Scrapbooking Made Simple

WE DO NOT REMEMBER **DAYS**; WE
REMEMBER **MOMENTS**. —*CESARE PAVESE*

When you think of scrapbooks, the word "simple" might not be the first thing that comes to mind. Perhaps you picture albums overflowing with pages of elaborate hand lettering, detailed decorations and photos in perfect chronological order. While there's nothing wrong with these albums, there are also many quick and easy scrapbook projects you can create—and I have twenty-five great ideas for you right here! My favorite thing about these meaningful projects is that they help you preserve what is most important and unique about you and your family. In this book, I'll guide you through the process of planning and compiling twenty-five entire albums that capture a specific aspect of your life—and you can make one in just a weekend!

YOU CAN "HAVE A LIFE" AND SCRAPBOOK TOO!

As a teacher, I meet thousands of scrapbook enthusiasts committed to the preservation of memories, but I also hear women say things like: "I just don't know where to start," "I have so many photographs that I'd never get caught up" or "I just don't have the time." I can relate! If I was just now beginning to scrapbook and walked into a scrapbook store, I think I would quite honestly turn around and run the other way. While it's very exciting to see this marvelous industry grow, the overwhelming proliferation of new products, ideas and information is just that—overwhelming!

I have a friend who emphatically proclaims herself a "non-scrap-booker." She tells me, "I admire the dedication of all the people I see involved in scrapbooking and I would probably do it too, but I have a life." There are many women like my friend for whom the thought of compiling a creative record of their life is completely

mind-boggling. They have so many boxes and drawers of pictures that it seems like a process that could potentially overtake every ounce of their free time as they attempt to "keep up" with it all.

Simple scrapbooks to the rescue! I'm here to show you how to quickly and easily record the most important aspects of your life—aspects that too often get left out of traditional scrapbooks—so you can still have time for all those other things in your life. There's a simple scrapbook in this book for everyone—from "non-scrapbookers" like my friend to dedicated scrapbook experts with several albums already under their belt.

WHY CREATE A SIMPLE SCRAPBOOK?

The need for creating simpler, more meaningful scrapbooks first became apparent to me a couple of years ago. A young mother came up to me after a design class I taught and eagerly asked if I would look through her scrapbooks and suggest how she might improve the design of her layouts. Even though I had been asked to

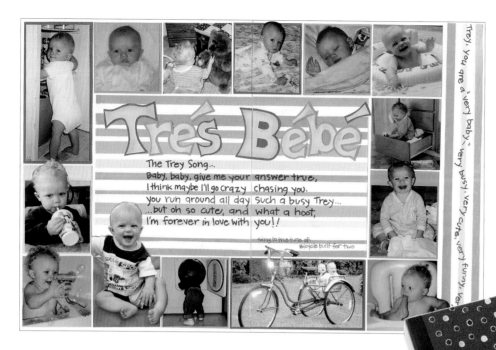

Tres Bebe

The Trey Song...
Baby, baby, give me your answer true,
I think maybe I'll go crazy chasing you.
You run around all day such a busy Trey...
...but oh so cute, and what a hoot,
I'm forever in love with you!!

sing to the tune of:
Bicycle built for two

"Tres Bebe" by Stacy Julian
Patterned Paper: Frances Meyer
Letter Stencil: Provo Craft
Idea to Note: Stacy found a French dictionary on the
internet and used it to look up words for her title.

for her family? What were her valued beliefs and traditions that she hoped to pass on to her children? I wondered if someone could look at my albums and also come away wanting to know more. Up until that point, I had justified the hours and hours I spent creating layouts with the knowledge that I was creating a record. But what if I wasn't preserving the information others would

Even though I had been asked to do similar evaluations in the past, this particular instance became a pivotal moment for me. This mother was completely caught up with her scrapbooks and had beautiful, well-designed layouts—everything I wished for myself. As I flipped through her two amazing scrapbooks, I saw page after page documenting nearly every event in her two-year-old's life, all presented in precise chronological order. Beginning with his trip home from the hospital, there were teddy bear pages, bath time pages and an orange popsicle page. She had documented trips to the zoo, the park and a parade. She had obviously devoted a great deal of time to this record. From a design standpoint, everything was in its place: photographs, titles, embellishments *and* names and dates. It was indeed impressive!

I closed the last album and gave her my glowing report, but I suddenly felt very empty. There was something missing. I wanted to know more. I could have easily turned to this devoted scrapbooker and, even after viewing both of her albums, asked her to tell me about life in her home. Oh, I knew about the events of the last two years—in great detail. But there was so much more I wanted to know. What about the routine of her daily life? What songs did she sing to her sons? What hopes and dreams did she have

really want to know? I knew then that I needed a new way to scrapbook—a way to truly capture the essence of my family and streamline the design process at the same time. And so began the evolution of simple scrapbooks.

WHAT IS A SIMPLE SCRAPBOOK?

A simple scrapbook is an album that focuses on one theme and follows a specific format with the help of a framework. Because there is so much about our lives and memories that we want to preserve, trying to do it all in one chronological album is quite overwhelming! Smaller, finite albums are not only easier to create and display, they are also easier for readers to digest and are therefore more likely to be enjoyed. A complete album that follows a pattern is generally more interesting than a never-ending project. While these kinds of albums may occasionally sacrifice chronological accuracy, the result will be much more meaningful.

This book then is not a collection of individual page

ideas, but rather of patterns for completed projects. For example, you'll learn how to create an album for each of your children that requires only a five-page update every year ("School of Life Scrapbook," p. 102), compile a scrapbook dedicated to the special relationships with your girlfriends ("Girlfriends Photo Book," p. 20) or capture the important aspects of your family's life in one beautiful display album ("Scrapbook of the Seasons," p. 56).

With the help of *Simple Scrapbooks*, you'll be able to write your own family story that acts as an index to all of your completed layouts and albums ("Family Storybook," p. 68). And after all this, you'll still have time to put together a "Pictures I Love" scrapbook pairing your favorite photographs with personal insights. It will become a priceless treasure to your children! I'm confident that this book has a project (or two) that appeals to you personally and can help you better preserve the meaningful aspects of your life.

THINKING BEYOND CHRONOLOGY

Theme scrapbooks are certainly not a new concept. Scrapbookers have traditionally been categorized

"My Favorite Photos" by Jeannie Ferderber
Album: Vineyard Mini Photo Album (5.25" x 7.25"), Kolo
Punches: Family Treasures
Computer Font: CK Journaling, "The Best of Creative Lettering" CD Vol. 2, *Creating Keepsakes*

according to how they work—chronologically or thematically. But have you ever thought of a chronological scrapbook as just one type of theme book, where the theme is the events of your life? When you bring home a roll of developed photographs, it's natural to sort them according to date and event—the birthday party, playing at the beach and so on. While this is a proven method, when it's the only type of organization used there's a good chance that important "non-event" memories will fall through the cracks. I recently created a layout about my grandmother's house that includes a journaling wheel revealing many of the happy memories I've had there. This is a way I captured non-event memories (see p. 13). What about the people you associate with and love, or the places you live, work, and visit often? What about your traditions, values and beliefs? All of these aspects need preserving, too. When you begin to see the events of your life as just one possible theme, other themes become quickly obvious.

In 1995, Peter Jennings and a team of journalists were given a massive five-year assignment to condense and capture the twentieth century in a twelve-hour television mini-series. They knew that since they were journalists—and not historians—they didn't want to try to cover every event or even present the information chronologically. Instead, they decided to approach the whole project from a story-telling standpoint, creating something more meaningful and interesting than a brief description of several events in each decade. The resulting series paired two stories in each episode—stories that perhaps seemed unrelated on the surface, but had some deeper connection.

The writers took events out of a sequential context and revisited them with the added benefit of their current perspective.

I was very taken with this series. As the family journalist, I decided to mimic some of these methods in my own scrapbooks. Shortly after watching "The Century" on television, I came across a photo of my grandfather kneeling next to my mother when she was very young. I immediately recognized a similarity between it and a photo in my baby book of my father kneeling next to me. I felt like Peter Jennings had given me permission to put these two photos on the same scrapbook page, even though they didn't belong together sequentially. I was thrilled with the outcome! In addition to the pictures, I included notes written by my mother and myself sharing some of our feelings for our "daddys." You can't look at this page and not contemplate the different generations and relationships that are represented on it. As I've started looking for these less-obvious connections and let my memories—and not just my photographs—dictate the themes I scrapbook, I have been able to sort and pre-

"Daddy's Little Girl" by Stacy Julian

Embossed Paper: Lasting Impressions for Paper

Pen: white writer by Pentel

Basket Die Cut: Heartland Paper Co.

Scissors (scallop edge): Family Treasures

Stamps (bees and flowers): Close To My Heart

Computer Font: CK Script, "The Best of Creative Lettering" Vol. 1, *Creating Keepsakes,* and CK Print "The Best of Creative Lettering" Vol. 2, *Creating Keepsakes.*

sent them in new and different ways. My creative "reporting" has really improved!

MAKING IT MEANINGFUL

One of my goals in writing this book is to help you learn how to recognize the important and meaningful aspects of your life that should be recorded. After the birth of my third son, I mentioned to my mother that I needed to find a good book on raising boys. She said,

"It's too bad you can't just sit down and talk to Minnie McDougal." My mother reminded me that Minnie, my great-grandmother, gave birth to ten sons! I guess she would know a thing or two about raising boys. Since I couldn't talk to Minnie, I turned to the family history records to see what I could learn. I was sorely disappointed. While I found a lot of dates, names, and places, I didn't find what I wanted. I wanted to know more about Minnie's relationships with those boys, her personality, her passions and her unique perspective on everyday life.

My daily life as a mother of boys is so very different from Minnie's, yet I am very much who she was. She is a part of me, having raised my grandpa, who raised my mom, who raised me. I have so many questions that I want to ask her. What did she do in her free time, if she had any? She must have read to my grandpa— he had such a thirst for knowledge and love of learning. What books did she love? Did she have girlfriends? How often did they get together? Stop and think about some of the things you wish you knew about your great-grand-

mother. Do your scrapbooks reveal these things about your own life? When we make a connection between our life and another person, place or time—as I did with Minnie—seemingly mundane moments become very meaningful. *Simple Scrapbooks* will help you make those meaningful connections as you narrow your focus and really develop a particular theme.

Gilbert and Minnie Hodge McDougal pictured with their first four sons about 1916 (below). All nine of the living McDougal boys (right). I love the comparison in size between the eldest (my grandfather) and the youngest, standing in front of him.

GETTING STARTED IN A WEEKEND:
BUILD THE FRAMEWORK

Many women mistakenly think that in order to begin scrapbooking, they have to have a designated scrapbook workspace, twenty-seven pairs of decorative scissors and files and files of patterned paper and stickers. At the very minimum, they assume they need to have their photographs sorted in chronological order. But all you really need to scrapbook is a weekend! In one weekend, you can build a framework for a simple scrapbook.

So what's a framework? A framework consists of a few pages that establish the organization, purpose and style of your album. It gives you a creative direction to follow as you fill in and later update your album with quick and easy pages. The parts of a framework include:

TITLE PAGE Every scrapbook needs a title page. Like the title page of a published book, the one for your scrapbook might include the name of the volume and your name as creator. You might also add a dedication or an explanation to your audience. The title page is also where you introduce the mood or feel of your album with particular colors, embellishments or design techniques. Because it's usually the first framework page you create, it also tends to be the most time-consuming as you decide the overall style for the rest of the album. Once the title page is complete and a design format is in place, the rest of the framework pages come together very quickly. Our Halloween scrapbook features one costume page for each child every year. It is a very fun way to capture their growth and interests over time.

TABLE OF CONTENTS A table of contents helps you establish the scope of your project: what topics your album is going to cover and in what order. You can be as specific or general as you like as you introduce the sections of your album. Not every scrapbook needs a table of contents.

SUBTITLE PAGES These pages introduce each section of your scrapbook (if you have more than one). They are usually similar in design to the title page. In addition to providing some organization to your album, these pages give the viewer a visual rest and chance to appreciate a section before venturing on. We have a section in our Halloween book dedicated to memories of the parties we host and attend.

FILL-IN PAGES These pages are the meat of your scrapbook. You don't have to create all of your fill-in pages at once. You might start with one or two pages for each section and then continue adding pages as your time permits. The fill-in pages usually tie in somehow with the design established by the title page, but how much "creative work" goes into each page is up to you. If you love the creative process of scrapbooking, this is where you can really have fun designing each page. If you're in a hurry, these pages can also be some of the fastest and easiest you create. Just follow a similar layout and repeat a design element, such as a border. The fill-in pages for "Costumes on Parade" are some of my most creative. I really have fun with these.

MATERIAL FILE I consider this part of a project's framework, but only you (the creator) will know about it. Once you decide on a theme for a simple scrapbook—and before you begin creating it—set up a file or place where you can begin to collect photographs, memorabilia, supplies and other materials you'll need. If your file is well prepared, your first weekend will be very productive! If you're compiling an album that will require occasional updates, this file can also serve as a place to store additional material waiting to be included.

With your framework in place at the end of the weekend, you'll have a wonderful sense of completion. Even if you still have fill-in pages to create for your album, the framework gives your project order and a sense of continuity. Once you've created a scrapbook using a framework, you'll never go back to doing it any other way!

HOW TO USE THIS BOOK

Simple Scrapbooks is divided into four chapters: Scrapbooks for Everyone, Scrapbooks for Families, Scrapbooks for Children, and Scrapbooks for the Holidays. With each project, I've shared a personal insight or story from my life, hoping that my experiences will trigger

"Halloween Book" by Stacy Julian
Metallic paper: source unknown
Stickers: Debbie Mumm
Letter Stencil: Pebbles in My Pocket
Other Stencils (star and square): Provo Craft
Sponging Ink: Close to My Heart

memories of your own and inspire you on to completion. The "Guidelines" section gives you specific details about what you need to compile a particular album and suggests ways to personalize and improve its overall meaning. Each project also features a "Preparation" sidebar to help you gather the information and supplies you'll need to successfully complete the scrapbook. And finally, in many cases you'll find variations of a project (created by other scrapbook designers) to help you envision ways you could adapt and personalize a project for your individual needs and style.

Don't feel you have to create scrapbooks that look just like the ones you see pictured in this book. I hope that you'll borrow some of my ideas and add some of your own to give your albums your own unique style. Once you select a project that you're interested in, think about it for several days to see how you could best adapt it to work for you. Then set up a materials file and begin collecting the information, photographs and products you'll need to begin. Mark off a weekend on your calendar (or two or three other days) and let everyone know you have a very important commitment. Finally, when the time comes—get busy! Before you know it, you'll have created a simple scrapbook. (Chronological scrapbookers: you'll be surprised at how liberating it feels!)

WEAVE YOUR OWN MEMORIES

Finally, my wish for you: whenever you create a scrapbook page, remember the underlying purpose of preserving your own unique memories for posterity. Not long ago on a Sunday morning, I arrived at church about ten minutes early. I sat down next to Edith, an 85-year-old woman, and asked her to share a favorite memory with me. She immediately began speaking of the long winter afternoons that she would spend sitting

"Grandma's House" by Stacy Julian
Patterned Paper: Close To My Heart
Stamps (strawberry and leaves): Close To My Heart
Flower Punch: Family Treasures
Template (for documenting wheel): Coluzzle square nested template, Provo Craft
Computer Font: Bernard Modern Roman
Idea to Note: Stacy included a documenting wheel (see cutout window in the corner of the photo) that turns and reveals several memories of her grandmother's house. Stacy resized and added text to photos using the Kodak Picture Maker.

at her mother's knee weaving rag rugs. She told me how she enjoyed those hours just being next to her mother and talking with her and listening to her. She asked me if I ever slowed down in my busy life. Did I ever just sit and in some way "weave"?

Edith's questions generated some serious introspection. There's no doubt that we live in a very fast-paced world. Women of our generation have so much to do. Yet I don't want to race through life and find that I've missed my share of quiet, everyday moments.

Later that same week, I found myself sitting for an hour or two in the hair salon, deep in thought. All of a sudden I realized that I was sitting and "weaving." Olga, my stylist, was "weaving" highlights into my hair! I felt a smile come to my face and I nearly laughed out loud. I decided that while I love hearing of simpler days gone by, I will probably never have the time or the need to weave rag rugs. To me, the word "weave" will always be what I have done to my hair every few months. I came to understand that my perspective on life is unique and important and needs preserving. I invite you to occasionally sit and "weave" your own unique perspective, personality and memories into a record that will really preserve who you are for your children and your children's children. Start today with a simple scrapbook!

"Stacy's Weave" by Stacy Julian
Patterned Paper: Hot Off The Press (weave); Frances Meyer (plaid)
Computer Fonts: Scrap Casual, Inspire Graphics; Hobo
Idea to Note: Stacy cut slits in the plaid paper and wove three strips of paper through the background.

Chapter 1

Scrapbooks for Everyone

THERE IS NO FENCE AROUND TIME THAT HAS GONE. **YOU CAN** GO BACK AND HAVE WHAT YOU LIKE IF YOU **REMEMBER** IT WELL ENOUGH. —RICHARD LLEWELLYN, *HOW GREEN WAS MY VALLEY*

I often hear people say "I'll start scrapbooking when I have kids. I don't really take enough pictures now to scrapbook." Let me be the first to tell you that you don't need to have children or even a lot of photographs stashed in boxes to begin compiling a scrapbook. The most important person you can scrapbook for is you, and the most important photos to put into a book may be the ones you haven't thought of taking yet.

The projects in this chapter will get you thinking about the unique and possibly forgotten aspects of your life that need to be recorded. What about your friendships? Your goals and dreams? What you like to do in your free time? Do you have a collection? Favorite recipes? Do you have special memories associated with your hometown or your encounters with nature?

Enough with the excuses. You don't need more time, more supplies, more creativity or even a child to begin scrapbooking. All you need are memories and an idea or two of how to "remember them well." That's what this book is here for.

IT'S TRUE THAT GREAT MEMORIES ARE often made at faraway locations, but some of my family's fondest memories are those that happen right in our own home when family and friends come to visit. We count down the days until our guests arrive and eagerly plan how we will spend the time they are with us. We love to recall the fun memories long after our guests are gone, but the details fade all to quickly. Fortunately, there's an easy way to capture and relive these much-anticipated visits. Create a guest book!

A guest book gives you a special place to chronicle all the people who have shared your home. Guests will look forward to "signing in" and you will have a colorful and personal record of each and every visit. Display your guest book near your main entry and everyone will enjoy browsing through it (especially if they're featured in it). Or, leave it on the night stand in your guest room with a vase of fresh flowers and a basket of goodies as a warm welcoming gesture.

While you may have already created scrapbook pages about particular guests in your regular family album, keeping a brief record of all your guests in one place makes for a fun and interesting smaller album. Don't feel like you have to go back and record all the visits that have already happened. If you want to include past visits, consider creating a collage of photos showing the people who have already come to stay and display it near the front of your book. Then start your guest book today, following the easy format here.

FUN IDEA A blank guest book makes a great house-warming gift for a new neighbor or a goodbye gift to friends who are moving away (suggesting they invite you to come for a visit!).

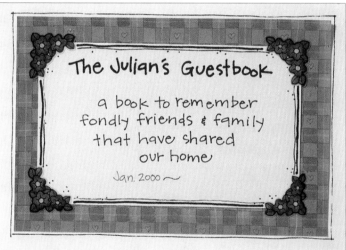

"Be Our Guest" by Stacy Julian

Album: 5" x 7" spiral-bound with canvas cover, Hiller
Letter Stencil: Pebbles Tracer, EK Success
Flower and Butterfly Stickers: Provo Craft
Patterned Paper: Julie Young
State Outline Computer Font: Mini Pics Boarderline Cutout
Star Punches: Marvy Uchida
Number Punches (used for "2000"): Family Treasures
Birthday Stickers: Me & My Big Ideas

It's true that great memories *are often made at faraway locations, but some of my family's* fondest *memories are those that happen right in our own home when family and friends* come to visit.

GUEST BOOK GUIDELINES

Creating a guest book is quick and easy! First, create the title page and decorate the cover if you want. Since my album had a canvas cover, I was able to add decorations directly to it. I used the title "Be Our Guest" and chose a decorating scheme of flowers and butterflies to use throughout the book. You can also have fun by introducing a particular theme like "The Smith's Retweet . . . everybirdies welcome." If you can't or don't want to decorate your album cover, simply include your title on the first page of the album. Also on the title page (or a subsequent subtitle page if you have small album pages), make sure you include your family's name and the date you began recording guest entries. You might want to also include the name of your hometown or a photo of your family or home, or a theme, such as the one suggested above.

Then, use two facing pages in your album to record each visit. On one page, leave a space for mounting a photo of the guest. Remember to take at least one picture during the visit. (If you don't have any photos from the featured visit, you can include a recent picture of the guest and indicate when and where the photo was

taken.) On the opposite page, mount a questionnaire that can be filled in by hand. Include several simple questions that provide a brief summary of the guest's visit. If you have a computer, you might want to type up your questionnaire so each page has a uniform appearance and you can easily print out a new copy whenever you need one. I used the five "W's" to formulate my questions:

- Who came to be our guest?
- When did they come?
- Where did they come from?
- Why did they come?
- What did we do?

After adding the photo and filling in the questionnaire, I like to add a few enhancements to the page that remind me of that particular visit. For example, I added birthday stickers to the page that features my parent's visit for my son's birthday. By using a similar placement (such as the lower right corner) or type of enhancement (sticker, die cut, stamp, etc.) on each page, you can give your album some continuity while still personalizing each page.

FUN IDEA If you frequently have out-of-state visitors, include a section in your guest book titled "Please sign in and 'state' your name." In this section, you can mount a small outline shape of the state the visitors came from and have them sign their name on that page. This is a fun way to see how many states you can feature in your book. My boys are already asking me to invite our friends from Colorado for a visit so we can add a new state to our collection!

PREPARATION

1 Purchase a small binder or spiral-bound album. I chose a 5" x 7" spiral-bound album for our family's guest book.

2 Choose coordinating stickers or other enhancements to decorate the cover and title page.

3 If you have a computer, you can type up a questionnaire form to mount opposite each photo. Then, you can print out a blank form whenever you need to add a new page, or even print out several and have your guest book pages ready and waiting to be filled in. (See Guidelines, p. 17, for question ideas.)

It's a great way to make your guests *feel even more* **welcome** *and important* *as they stay* in your home.

BECKY HIGGINS HAS CREATED A GUEST BOOK that also features two pages per visit—one with a photo and the facing page with a journal entry. In Becky's book, however, she invites her guests to fill out the form about their visit themselves (before they leave), including information such as where they traveled from and highlights of their visit. This format lets your guests provide their own version of their visit and gives you a great way to record their handwriting as well! Then, she color coordinates the page decorations around the photo.

You'll find that a guest book is quick and easy to update with each visit—and it's a great way to make your guests feel even more welcome and important as they stay in your home.

"Be Our Guest"
by Becky Higgins
Album: 8" x 8" spiral-bound
Mrs. Grossman's
Computer Font (guest journal entry): CK Anything Goes "The Best of Creative Lettering" CD Vol. 1, *Creating Keepsakes*

FRIENDS COME AND GO THROUGHOUT our lives. Sometimes people we think we'll never forget can fade in our memories. One day as I was looking through my mother's wedding album, I came to a photo of the bridesmaids and I asked her to tell me about them. Of the five women pictured, my mom could only remember three full names! These were the women that she hand-picked to share one of the most important days of her life; these were the ones that were willing to dress alike and stand in those very uncomfortable shoes for hours on end. While some of their memories and stories are still clear to her, many are not.

I want my children to know how important my friends have been to me and to learn a little about them. At the same time, I want a place to celebrate these women and my relationships with them. One way to capture these valued relationships is by creating a girlfriends photo book. In this book, your special friends are highlighted in different sections, which can be expanded throughout the years with updated photos and other keepsakes. The result is an album that helps tell the stories of the friendships you've treasured throughout your life.

A girlfriends book can be used to highlight friendships from all aspects and times of your life. You can include childhood and college friends, friendships formed through associations such as church and clubs, or simply your neighbor friends. In addition to capturing your more casual friendships and associations, this book is a wonderful place to really feature those extra-special friendships. I knew right off that I wanted to highlight

"My Girlfriends Book" by Stacy Julian

Album: Black leather, Dalee Book Co.

Metallic Sticker Letters: Pebbles in My Pocket

Metallic Paper: Paper Adventures

Punches: Large sun, large and small star, Family Treasures

Pens: Gold/Silver Hybrid Gel Roller, Pentel; Zig Millennium 08 and 03, EK Success

Computer Font: CK Journaling, "The Best of Creative Lettering" CD Vol. 2, *Creating Keepsakes*

Angel Stamp: Close to My Heart

Small Sticker Letters (used for "Stamping"): Making Memories

Make new friends
but keep the old

one is silver
and
the other's gold.

Created by Stacy Julian
and dedicated to the women I adore.

I want my children to know how important *my* friends *have been to me and to know a little more about them. I want a place to* celebrate *these women and my relationships with them.*

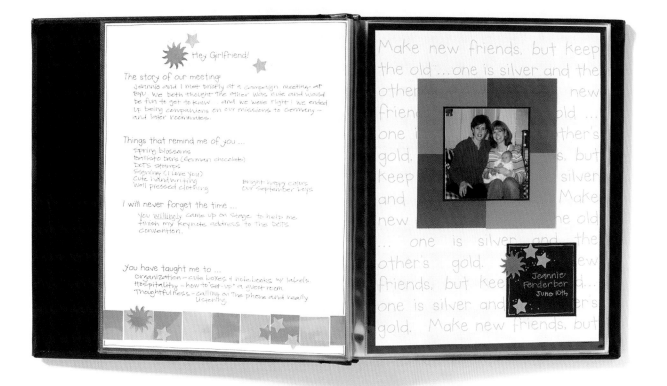

Hey Girlfriend!

The story of our meeting:
Jeannie and I met briefly at a campaign meeting at BYU. We both thought the other was cute and would be fun to get to know ... and we were right! We ended up being companions on our missions to Germany — and later roommates.

Things that remind me of you ...
Spring blossoms
Brilliato bars (German chocolate)
DOTS stamps
Signing (I Love You)
Cute handwriting
Well pressed clothing
Bright happy colors
our September boys

I will never forget the time ...
You willingly came up on stage to help me finish my keynote address to the DOTS convention.

You have taught me to ...
Organization — cute boxes & notebooks w/ labels.
Hospitality — how to "set up" a guest room.
Thoughtfulness — calling on the phone and really listening.

Jeannie Ferderber
June 10th

my relationship with Jeannie Ferderber—one of my very best friends (you know, the call-on-the-phone-every-day type). While Jeannie and I only shared one year together as college roommates, we have managed to stay very close in the passing years even though we've lived quite far apart. What better way to celebrate a treasured friend like Jeannie than in a special girlfriends book!

GIRLFRIENDS BOOK GUIDELINES

First, create a title page for your overall album. I chose the title "My Girlfriends Book" and also created a subtitle page to introduce my selected theme: *Make new friends but keep the old; one is silver and the other's gold.* To enhance this theme and lend a contemporary feel, I used gold and silver metallic squares, sun and star punches throughout the book; I chose black as my neutral color.

Next, create a separate section for each girlfriend you want to highlight. Each section will begin with a two-page spread (p. 21). On the right page, include a photo of your girlfriend and yourself together, along with her name and birthday. On the left page, mount a questionnaire that includes three or four of the questions from the bulleted list. You can simply write the question and answer (as I did), or you might want to use the questions as a starting point for an essay-type page describing your relationship with this friend. Don't feel like you have to use all of these questions for each friend—simply select three or four that help you best describe your relationship. You might even want to use different questions for different friends.

- How and when did you meet?
- How are you alike and how are you different?
- What hobbies and interests do you share?
- What do you talk about when you're together?
- What have you learned from this friend?
- What prompts you to get together with, call or e-mail this friend?

Make a list of your best girlfriends that you want to celebrate—include childhood, college, and adult friends.

Round up two or three photos of each friend.

Select three or four questions to answer for each relationship (suggestions given in Guidelines).

Select and purchase an album for your book—I chose an 8.5" x 11" post-bound album.

Choose a theme and a neutral color to use throughout your book.

- Describe a memorable experience you've shared.
- What things (flowers, music, stores, places, restaurants, etc.) remind you of this friend?
- What is a favorite card or gift you've given to or received from this friend?

Following each introductory spread, insert as many single "fill-in" pages as you need for that friend's section. These pages can include items such as wedding and baby announcements, children's photos, letters and notes, updated photos and so on. You can be as creative as you like with the fill-in page layouts, but I tend to keep mine very simple with only a few enhancements so that the task of updating my book isn't a major ordeal. Each girlfriend's fill-in section will grow with time. Remember that it's not necessary to include *all* of your photos and keepsakes for each friend. Being selective and choosing the most memorable items will strengthen the overall book.

You can also create a pocket page for each girlfriend's section where you can store photos and memorabilia from that friend until you're ready to update your book. The pocket page can also hold keepsake items related to that friend that aren't easily mounted directly onto a page. In addition, I like to use my pocket pages to hold items such as cards that I find or make and want to send to one of my girlfriends. I just slip it inside that friend's pocket until it's time to send it.

FUN IDEA The outside of pocket pages are great places to feature favorite quotes (p. 22). I love to include quotes in my albums.

Finally, you can include an "Other Women I Adore" section at the end of your girlfriends book to briefly feature some of the other friends you've met and associated with through the years. In this section, simply create one or two pages for each friend. Include the friend's name, a photo (if available) and a short written comment describing your relationship. In addition, you can create collage pages that highlight special groups of friends. I've done this in my book for groups such as stamping and scrapbooking friends, couple friends we met in school, co-workers from jobs I've had, book club or play group members, and so on.

FUN IDEA If your friends are spread out, include a page with a map that pinpoints where all your long distance friends live!

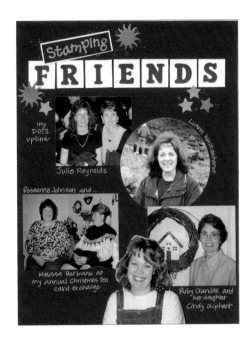

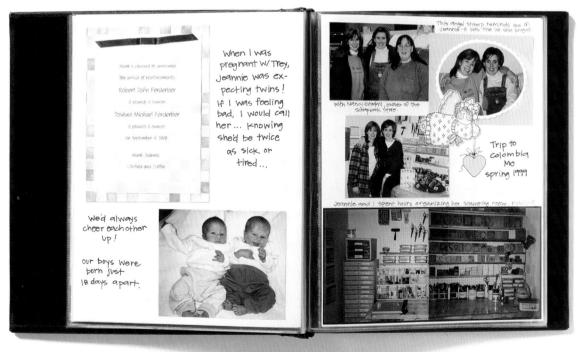

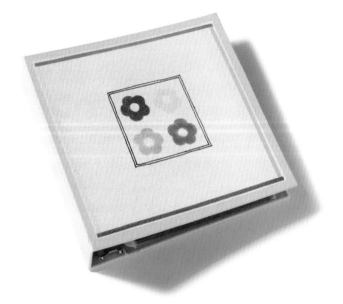

THERE ARE MANY WAYS YOU CAN ADAPT this project to feature relationships other than just girlfriends. Jenny Jackson has created a wonderful variation that she titled "The Jackson Family Big Book of Family Friends." Jenny divided her friends into four groups—family friends, school friends, church friends and babysitting group. She chose the theme "Friends are the flowers in the garden of life" and selected bright, fun colors. Jenny strengthened her theme by using a simple flower stamp throughout her book. She chose a different color for each of the four sections, but using the same stamp helped give her book a strong feeling of continuity.

Jenny created a title page, a table of contents listing the four groups of friends and the color associated with each group, and a subtitle page for each section with a large flower in the selected color. Then, within each section, she created as many pages as needed to highlight her family's friendships. She kept the page layout simple and consistent—a background created with her flower stamp in various colors, and a few stronger page elements (such as paper strips) in the featured color for each section. This way, she didn't need to spend a lot of time on each page. Each section can easily be updated and expanded in the future as needed.

FUN IDEA Another fun variation would be to use a similar format to highlight relationships with family members such as siblings or nieces and nephews. Create a fun cousins book for your children to highlight the special relationships they have with their cousins, or to help them get to know those family members they don't get to see very often. You could create a grandchildren's book featuring the grandchildren divided into families—what a wonderful gift that's sure to be cherished by any grandparent!

A girlfriends photo book gives you a place to keep track of and remember all the wonderful friendships you've forged over the years. And friendships are something definitely worth remembering!

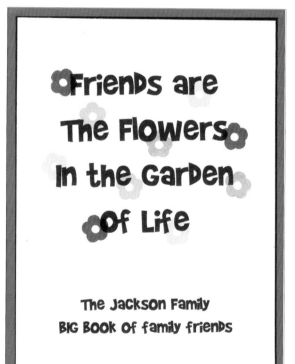

"The Jackson Family Big Book of Family Friends" by Jenny Jackson

Spring Blossom Stamp: Close To My Heart

Paper and Inks: Close To My Heart

Computer Font: Unknown

Large Flower: Jenny's own design (inspired by the stamp)

Family Friends

School Friends

Church Friends

Babysitting Group

Babysitting Group

Another fun variation would be to use a similar format to **highlight** *relationships with* family members *such as siblings or nieces and nephews.*

In August 1997, we created our Babysitting Group. It was the greatest thing we ever did! We had 4 families for a total of 6 kids. The Salmons, the Jacobsens, the Whipples & the Jacksons. We each took one Friday per month and dropped the kids off for "date night." So we endured 4 hours of craziness and enjoyed 3 weekends of dates! It doesn't get any better than this! And the kids love to be together. They look forward to it as much as we do.

JR. & Joe Salmons

Laura Jacobsen

Sarah Whipple

Hopes and Wishes Book

DO YOU REMEMBER WHAT YOU WANTED out of life when you graduated from college? Got married? Retired? My sister Darci is a very motivated, goal-oriented person and knows what she wants to accomplish in life. When she recently got married (one of her lifelong dreams), she realized that there was now another person to include in her goal planning. Knowing that goals are most effective when they're recorded, she and her new husband sat down together and wrote some hopes and dreams for their future. While many couples create such a list, Darci went a step further and recorded their dreams in a fun little "Hopes and Wishes" scrapbook.

A hopes and wishes book can capture both the serious and the more silly goals you have for yourself (and your spouse). Most importantly, it gives you a special place to not only keep track of your goals but also to celebrate them when they happen. It also gives posterity a unique perspective on what was important to you at a particular stage in your life—and gives you perspective as to whether your priorities and dreams changed. How interesting it would be to know what things your great-grandmother thought she wanted from life when she was just starting out, and then to compare those early goals to what she did with the hand life actually dealt her! Even more meaningful would be to have her comments and insights about her goals as she accomplished them. This project can be created at any time in life, but it lends itself especially well to times of new beginnings such as graduations, marriages, retirements and so on.

This is a perfect beginning project for a new scrapbooker—you don't even need any photos to get started! A little book like this also serves as a great checklist and journal for those special vacations and other one-time events. Write down your "before" expectations and see what happens!

"Someday... A Book of Hopes and Wishes" by Darci Dowdle

Album: Century Photo Products

Stickers: Suzy's Zoo

Patterned Paper: Paper Patch (dedication page, school spread, green paper on garden spread); Provo Craft (dog spread); Frances Meyer (garden paper on garden spread)

Ruler Frame: My Mind's Eye

When I was a girl I hoped that
Someday...

I would grow up and get married
Well, I did...

So ... Now What?

I have created this little book
and dedicated it to my sweetheart,
as a place to
celebrate and record our goals, and our
together
wishes and dreams.

so that someday
we can share them with our children.

The Dowdles
November 28, 1999

Knowing that goals
are most effective when
they're recorded,
she and her new
husband sat down
together *and wrote some*
hopes and dreams for
their future.

HOPES AND WISHES BOOK GUIDELINES

Begin your book by creating a title page and a dedication spread. On these pages, include the name of the person (or people) writing the goals (include a photo if you can), the date the goals were initially recorded and the reasons or motivations for compiling the book. Darci titled her book simply "Someday...," with a subtitle of "A Book of Hopes and Wishes." She carried the "Someday..." theme throughout the dedication and individual goal pages.

Then, you'll create a two-page spread for each wish or goal. On one page, write the actual goal and leave space for a photo that you can later include of the goal being accomplished. On the other page, mount a questionnaire form where you can answer some questions about completing your goal. The form should include a space for the date and place the goal was completed, as well as your comments on reaching the goal. You might include questions such as:

- Was achieving this goal everything you thought it would be?
- Did it take the amount of time you thought it would?
- Would you do it again?
- What was the hardest part?
- What was the biggest reward in realizing this goal?
- Who is the most proud or excited?

Finally, decorate your pages so your book is ready to celebrate each of your accomplishments. Darci chose to decorate her book with Suzy's Zoo stickers (her favorite in the whole world). After making her initial list of goals, she purchased several stickers that would work well to enhance each goal. Then, she worked with the colors of the stickers to select cardstock and patterned paper for each spread, leaving a blank area for a completion photograph. The result is a very fun, inviting book with a lot of visual appeal—and it was whipped up in a jiffy!

FUN IDEA Add even more meaning to your book by including a page at the back of the book with a photo of your parents or grandparents and a list of five things that they consider to be their most important or memorable accomplishments in life.

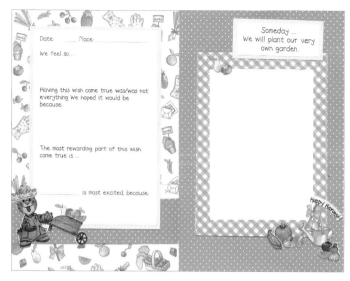

PREPARATION

1 Make a list of 15-20 things you'd like to accomplish in your life. Include serious and not-so-serious goals, like having a child, traveling to a specific place, buying a home, making a really good rhubarb pie, getting a job, earning a promotion, meeting someone you admire, reading a certain book, or living to see a particular technological advancement or event.

2 Purchase some page embellishments that you can use throughout your album to unify your overall design, such as a particular line of stickers, a set of rubber stamps, or two or three similar punches.

3 Create a questionnaire form to use with each goal that will be filled out upon reaching the goal. If you have a computer, you can type up the questionnaire form and then easily print out as many as you need. (See Guidelines, p. 27, for suggested questions.)

4 Purchase a small album for your book. Darci selected a small three-ring binder that holds 5.5" x 8.5" pages.

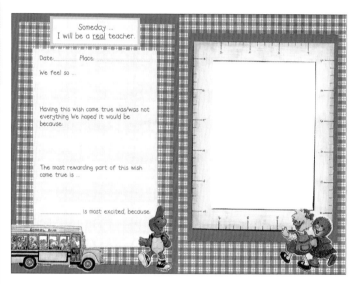

"Our Retirement Album" by Pam Talluto

Album: Generations by Hazel

Circle Punches: Family Treasures

Computer Fonts: CK Wedding and CK Journaling, "The Best of Creative Lettering" CD Vol. 2, *Creating Keepsakes*

Rose Stickers: Unknown

PAM TALLUTO CREATED A LITTLE RETIREMENT album as a gift for her parents to help them record and accomplish their dreams for retirement. She simply created the title page and a two-page spread featuring a photo and a checklist of things they always talk about doing. Now they have a place to record some of their long-awaited dreams.

Another variation of this book that is especially fun for retirement is to create a little travel wish book of places you'd like to see. You might include a postcard or picture of each place or landmark, then mount a photo of you there alongside it when it happens!

So take that first step and write down your goals and dreams. Then go a step further and record them in a fun hopes and wishes book. It can be a great source of inspiration as you (and your family members) are reminded often of what you want to accomplish in life, and it will be a wonderful celebration of your achievements!

FOOD, GLORIOUS FOOD! ISN'T IT INTERESTING how something as simple as food can evoke such strong memories and emotions? No matter what our cultural heritage is, we frequently associate certain foods with particular events, traditions, people, places and so on. Foods that remind us of home provide comfort when we're away. Family recipes are passed down for generations, often accompanied by practical tips and heartwarming stories. But too often, those stories and memories fade from one generation to the next.

When my mother-in-law passed away just two years after I was married, I was given a book containing several family recipes. I've tried the recipe for Grandma Grant's chocolate cake once or twice, but I know I'm missing the key ingredient—and it's not the buttermilk. It's the memories. I wish I knew where Grandma got her recipe. I'd sure like to know her secret for the cooked icing—I've yet to get it right! I wonder who considered this their favorite dessert? Which special occasions did she bake it for?

As a gift for my sister's bridal shower last year, I decided to compile a small "Book of Family Recipes" for her. I wanted the book to focus on specific memories associated with each family recipe so they wouldn't be forgotten. I asked each person to send several special recipes, along with some thoughts and comments about their submissions. The resulting family recipe book is a wonderful collection of not only delicious recipes and special preparation tips and tricks but also, and most importantly, precious family memories and traditions. A family recipe album makes a gift that's sure to be cherished by a new bride or a child leaving home for the first time. Or, simply create one for yourself and start today to preserve some of your family's rich heritage.

FUN IDEA Your recipe album doesn't have to be limited to family recipes. You could create a collection of recipes from neighbors, co-workers or a group of special friends.

"Book of Family Recipes" by Stacy Julian

Album: 6" x 6" post-bound, Close to My Heart

Patterned Paper: Close to My Heart

Scissors: Jumbo Pinking edge, Family Treasures

Computer Font: CK Journaling, "The Best of Creative Lettering" CD Vol. 2, *Creating Keepsakes*; Other, Unknown

Recipe Card and Kitchen Stamps: Close to My Heart

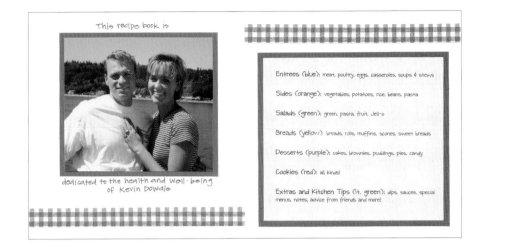

This recipe book is

dedicated to the health and well-being of Kevin Dowdle

Entrees (blue): meat, poultry, eggs, casseroles, soups & stews

Sides (orange): vegetables, potatoes, rice, beans, pasta

Salads (green): green, pasta, fruit, Jell-o

Breads (yellow): breads, rolls, muffins, scones, sweet breads

Desserts (purple): cakes, brownies, puddings, pies, candy

Cookies (red): all kinds!

Extras and Kitchen Tips (lt. green): dips, sauces, special menus, notes, advice from friends and more!

Taken at City Creek Canyon

Salt Lake City, UT   Thanksgiving 1997

Macaroni & Cheese
Chanda Hall

This is my favorite "in a hurry, soft on the tummy" meal. It reminds me of Summer days by the pool and games of Monopoly on the livingroom floor. Some say you can cut up hot dog bits to add meat, but the simplicity of M&C is what is so great if you ask me. I am sharing this recipe with you because you come from a long line of Hall women who think if it's not from scratch it's no good. I'm here to tell you that you have so many talents that you will find yourself very busy quite often. Don't let yourself get overwhelmed at mealtime by feeling you "have to" make a glorious meal from scratch. With M&C the kids are always happy. Food comes and goes, but time is precious. Lastly, don't buy the Costco brand. I highly recommend Kraft or Mission – the rest just don't compare. ♡

I've tried the recipe *for Grandma Grant's chocolate cake once or twice, but I know I'm missing the key* ingredient— *and it's not the buttermilk. It's the* memories.

GATHERING RECIPES

The biggest task in creating a recipe album is gathering the recipes and memories from family members or friends. For my sister Darci's book, I sent out a letter to members from both sides of the family and asked them to send me four or five special recipes. I requested that the recipes be handwritten on 3" x 5" cards, and I also asked each person to include some thoughts about each recipe.

To help me get back the type of information I wanted for each recipe, I included a list of questions with my letter. However, I noted that the person shouldn't feel like they had to answer every question. Instead, I hoped the questions would spark the person's memories and allow them to more easily think of anecdotes about each recipe. Here are some possible questions:

- Whose recipe is this? Who in your family makes this most often, or who is associated most strongly with this recipe? Where did it originate (another family, country, etc.)?
- Whose favorite recipe is this? Why?

Ginger Bunny Cookies
Connie Hall/Stacy Julian

This is mom's recipe, but I'm contributing it, because I love making them so much. I think "Ginger Bunnies" are a Connie Hall original — you grow up thinking everyone has a bunny cookie in their Easter basket with their name on it .. and then you learn the truth and realize once again what a cool and special mother you have. This is a wonderful holiday tradition. Tip: If you live somewhere dry, store your extra bunnies in an airtight container — to help keep them soft. ♡

Oatmeal Cookies
Addie Hall

All the Hall boys like these! The secret to these cookies is steaming the raisins and adding dates and nuts too. The combination of spices make them prize winners! ♡

about 1948

Briggs   Glade   Brent   Suzanne

• Are there any funny stories surrounding this particular recipe?
• Is there a special kitchen tool that should be used when making this recipe or a special kind of dish it should be served in? Are there other foods that should be served with this recipe?
• Is there a special or secret ingredient, something homegrown or something acquired at a specialty store?
• Is there a certain time of year your family most enjoys this recipe? Do you make it for a particular holiday, birthday or other celebration?
• Was this recipe ever served at a memorable occasion (baby shower, graduation, wedding, etc.)?

RECIPE ALBUM GUIDELINES

Once you've gathered your recipes, you're ready to begin your album. At the beginning of your recipe book, create a title page, dedication page and a table of contents. On the title page, include the person or family's name (or indicate the source of the recipes, such as a neighborhood collection). The dedication page gives you a place for a photo and either a short, fun dedication like I used in Darci's book or a more descriptive entry of your reasons behind collecting the recipes. On the table of contents page, list each of the sections for your book. Darci's book includes entrees, side dishes, salads, breads, desserts and cookies. Rather than give

Recipe for Happiness
Addie Hall

Happiness Recipe
Take equal parts of kindness,
unselfishness & thoughtfulness.
Mix in an atmosphere
of love.
Add a spice of usefulness.
Scatter a few grains of
cheerfulness. Season with
smiles and serve to
everybody. Love, Grandma

page numbers for each section, I indicated the color I used for decorating pages in that section. I tried to simplify the overall design of the book by using just two different types of checked patterned paper (in several colors) throughout the book.

Next, create a subtitle page spread for the beginning of each section (in the associated color). On the left page, I included a blank space for a photo so Darci can later personalize her book with photos from her own kitchen and family gatherings. On the right page, include the title of the section.

Within each section, list the title of each recipe, the name of the person submitting the recipe and the memories, tips or comments from that person. Some pages will feature two or three recipes and some only one, depending on how much information you received and whether or not you have a photo to include. To make the page layouts quick and easy, as well as give some continuity to the entire book, I decorated each recipe page with just a strip of patterned paper (in the appropriate section color) along either the top or bottom of the page, depending on whether it was a left or right-hand page.

You might notice that the actual recipes are not mounted on the album pages. Instead, the recipe cards are tucked inside the page protectors between each set of back-to-back pages. Again, this places the emphasis on the memories instead of on the ingredients. Also, doing this gives you the freedom of removing the recipe cards and filing them in a separate box if you prefer.

Lastly, include some photos throughout the recipe pages. You might use a picture of the prepared recipe if you have one available, or just a photo of a person, place or event that has something to do with that particular recipe. Photo captions add even more of a personal touch!

FUN IDEA Why not add a bonus section to your recipe book: kitchen tips and tricks! You might include a photo of all the "cooks" that have contributed recipes to your book, with a tip or two from each. See the "Recipe for Happiness" from Grandma Hall.

Being able to prepare balanced meals is admirable, but a recipe album like this helps make sure that you and your family will always be able to "cook up" some really delicious family memories!

PREPARATION

1 Decide where your recipes will come from—immediate or extended family, co-workers, friends, etc.

2 Make a list of recipe categories you want to include. You might do a complete book like I did, or specialize in a certain food category such as cookie recipes ("The best, most yummiest cookie recipes I know") or picnic foods ("Life's a picnic").

3 Begin gathering recipes in each category. (See Gathering Recipes, p. 31).

4 Choose a color to use for each recipe category, and purchase patterned paper or other embellishments in each color.

5 Select and purchase a small album. I used a post-bound 6"x 6" album.

Corn Casserole
Stacy Julian

We were newly married, living in Chicago and I was wishing I could be at home for Thanksgiving – but instead we went to the Miller's in Mitchell Indiana for dinner. When I tasted this, I realized that everyone thinks their family does Thanksgiving just right and everyone has recipes that are "must-haves". It would be my job to "mesh" the best of two great families and come up with our own Julian menu. I'm passing it on to you, because it is now a tradition at our table and a very delicious one at that! It is from Geof's grandma Ruth Julian. ♡

Pure Gold!
24 "carrot" kids
fresh carrots from
Grandpa's garden
October '99

Yummy Baked Carrots
Stacy Julian

I just love these. They are so easy to make and so delicious for Sunday dinner or a side to any "nicer" meal. Just use those bags of baby carrots and make sure you splurge and use "real" butter – you'll be glad you did. Chase "hates" cooked carrots – but he likes these. ♡

MY FRIEND SHARON SONEFF COLLECTS TEA cups and serving pieces. Her beautiful collection started several years ago with a birthday gift of a hand-painted vintage tea cup, and her collection now has more than 60 pieces! Sharon loves the "treasure hunt" aspect of finding new tea cups and regularly puts her collection to use for elegant birthday teas and bridal and baby showers.

Do you have a collection? Most collectors have a strong emotional attachment to their collection and many happy memories surrounding each piece. Because there are so many stories behind a collection, a scrapbook is the perfect place to record them and the associated memories. Imagine inheriting a great-grandparent's collection accompanied by a book full of pictures, memories and other details describing the collection's history and meaning. What a wonderful treasure! So whatever you collect—dolls, dishes, quilts or even apples—preserve it today in your very own collector's catalogue!

FUN IDEA If you know someone with a prized collection, create a blank book for them (leaving spaces for photos and memories), with a personal plea for them to complete it. Or, give a child a blank little album and a disposable camera. Let them take pictures of their treasures and mount them next to their own words about each item.

PHOTOGRAPHY TIPS

Unless you're in the habit of shooting still-life photography, you probably don't have very many pictures

"Tea Anthology Album" by Sharon Soneff

Album: 8.5" x 11" tapestry binder, Hiller

Embossed Floral Frames, Photo Corners and Adhesive Borders: "Scrapbook Beautiful," K & Company

Tea Stamps: The Holly Pond Hill collection, Uptown Rubber Stamps

Pen: Pigma Micron, Sakura

Computer Font: Harrington

Idea to Note: The embossed floral frames make creating the title and section subtitle pages quick and easy while providing a consistent look.

of your collection. So the first thing you'll need to do is to set up a photo shoot!

Here are a few tips for photographing your collection:
- Use natural light.
- Fill the frame with the object.
- Create a pleasing backdrop.
- Arrange the pieces so you can see them best and add accessory items to create a more pleasing setting.
- Include yourself in a few of the photos—you are a very important part of this collection!
- If you have a large collection with a lot of pieces, consider grouping similar or related items together in one photo rather than shooting each piece individually. Save the individual photos for pieces that have the most meaning to you or a particularly interesting story behind them.
- Take a picture or two showing how you normally display or store your entire collection.

Most collectors have a strong emotional *attachment to their collection and many* happy memories *surrounding each piece.*

FUN IDEA

Color copying (or scanning) is a useful alternative to photographing some types of collections. For example, you could "picture" parts of a quilt collection by color copying a section of each quilt, then reducing it to the size you need. This is also a great method for showing close-ups and detail of certain items.

COLLECTOR'S CATALOGUE GUIDELINES

At the beginning of your scrapbook, include a title page that indicates the name of the collector, the type of item collected and the date the album was created. Try to select colors and other materials that reflect the theme or style of the collection. Sharon Soneff has created a beautiful scrapbook titled "Tea Anthology Album" about her teacup collection. Sharon's title page immediately sets a mood of simple elegance for her album by introducing soft colors and embellishments such as embossed paper and Victorian tea stamps. Sharon also used similar design elements throughout her album to give it some consistency. She bordered each page with an embossed, scalloped edged strip and matted her photographs with simple, narrow mats and an occasional embossed corner. (Looking through her book is like sitting down to an afternoon tea—you feel calm, relaxed and just a bit extravagant!)

The next step is to decide how you want to organize your album. To help in this process, first think about the following:

- Why you collect what you do and how your collection got started.
- Places you've visited to add to your collection.
- Special people you've met or associated with because of your collection.
- Whether your collection is just decorative or functional and how you display or use it.

You can use this information to help determine sections of your album. For example, if you have traveled a lot to add to your collection, you could create an entire section about the places you've visited. Or, you might simply create an introductory page or spread that con-

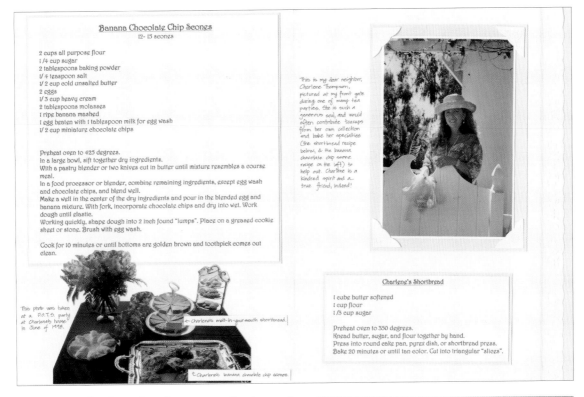

Banana Chocolate Chip Scones
12- 15 scones

2 cups all purpose flour
1/4 cup sugar
2 tablespoons baking powder
1/4 teaspoon salt
1/2 cup cold unsalted butter
2 eggs
1/3 cup heavy cream
2 tablespoons molasses
1 ripe banana mashed
1 egg beaten with 1 tablespoon milk for egg wash
1/2 cup miniature chocolate chips

Preheat oven to 425 degrees.
In a large bowl, sift together dry ingredients.
With a pastry blender or two knives cut in butter until mixture resembles a course meal.
In a food processor or blender, combine remaining ingredients, except egg wash and chocolate chips, and blend well.
Make a well in the center of the dry ingredients and pour in the blended egg and banana mixture. With fork, incorporate chocolate chips and dry into wet. Work dough until elastic.
Working quickly, shape dough into 2 inch found "lumps". Place on a greased cookie sheet or stone. Brush with egg wash.

Cook for 10 minutes or until bottoms are golden brown and toothpick comes out clean.

This is my dear neighbor, Charlene Thompson, pictured at my front gate during one of many tea parties. She is such a generous soul, and would often contribute teacups from her own collection and bake her specialties (the shortbread recipe below, & the banana chocolate chip scone recipe on the left) to help out. Charlene is a kindred spirit and a true friend, indeed!

This photo was taken at a P.O.T.S. party at Charlene's home in June of 1998.

← Charlene's melt-in-your-mouth shortbread.

← Charlene's banana chocolate chip scones.

Charlene's Shortbread

1 cube butter softened
1 cup flour
1/3 cup sugar

Preheat oven to 350 degrees.
Knead butter, sugar, and flour together by hand.
Press into round cake pan, pyrex dish, or shortbread press.
Bake 20 minutes or until tan color. Cut into triangular "slices".

tains a little history and information about your collection, as I did for my apple collection album.

Sharon's love of hosting tea parties led her to create several sections in her tea album in addition to the one featuring her tea cup photos. She created a table of contents that divides her book into four different sections: Favorite Tea Cups & Accoutrements, Favorite Tea Time Recipes, Favorite Tea Party Memories and Favorite Hints for a Successful Tea. These categories reflect the activities and memories that Sharon associates with her collection.

When you create the pages featuring the pieces of your collection, remember to label each photo clearly and include information such as when you acquired that piece and any interesting stories associated with it. If you have a large collection, consider creating pages only for your favorite pieces, rather than highlighting each individual item. Then, include a page with a photo or two of the entire collection. You might also want to group the photographs according to categories such as gifts received, items purchased on special trips, and so on.

FUN IDEA Include a tally list of all the items in your collection, or even a log where you can record each new item as you add it, indicating whether it was a gift, a souvenir or a long-awaited purchase.

No matter what you collect or how big your collection is, creating a collector's catalogue is a fun way to showcase it. (Just think how easy it will be to share your collection with those who can't come see it in person!) And you'll also be adding a very important "piece" to your collection—the stories and memories behind it!

PREPARATION

1 Take some pictures of your collection! (See Photography Tips, p. 34.)

2 Decide on the "feel" and color scheme you'd like your album to have. Purchase several sheets of paper and decorative elements to enhance your photographs. Try to complement the style of your collection.

3 Choose and purchase an album if needed. Sharon used an 8.5" x 11" tapestry album for her tea collection and I chose a 6" x 9" album for my apple collection.

the rest of
My Collection

I love fruit themes (particularly grapes, berries, plums, & pears) so naturally I was drawn to these English, fine china tea cups. I purchased both of them at a discount store (Marshall's). The one shown at the right is by Royal Nobita and the one below is by Duchess.

Another teacup gifted to me by my sister, Lisa, & her husband Serge, was this beautiful embossed fine china cup & saucer (at right) with a pansy motif. It is by Crown Dorset & it is made in England. They found it on their honeymoon (March 1996) while in a china shop in Victoria, British Columbia. The similar cup (below) is also a treasured birthday gift from my friend, Joanne Johnson. Also a pansy motif. (Those who know me, know I love all things purple!) It was made by Duchess. This was my first set to suffer a casualty; shortly after this photo was taken, the saucer was broken while cleaning. It still is a lovely cup by itself.

"Life is a cup
to be filled,
not drained"
Anonymous

Back Row—
Alex Perry,
Cynthia,
Me,
Denise Rice,
Patti Shambrook,
Kristi McCormick

Front Row—
Wendy Macadam,
Janelle Simons
(the birthday girl), and
Becky Salazar

Birthday Brunch & Tea
Honoring Janelle Simons

On the lower deck of our San Clemente home, we basked in the sun & in the beauty of friendship and the beauty of nature.

On this sunny morning in May of 1997, a group of friends gathered for morning brunch & tea at my home to celebrate & honor our dear friend Janelle Simons. The hours spent that morning were unforgettable & dear as we enjoyed one another, delicious food & tea, and the beauty surrounding us on all sides. This was one of those parties that fell together at the last minute with almost no planning, and yet with all the planning in the world we could not duplicate the treasured moments of that day.

"Somehow taking tea together encourages an atmosphere of intimacy when you slip off the timepiece in your mind and cast your fate to a delight of tasty tea, tiny foods, and thoughtful conversation.
Gail Greco

FOR ME, IT ALL STARTED WITH A MARRIAGE proposal, a small country store and two apple mugs. My apple collection, that is. I was newly engaged when I saw the mugs while shopping with my mom. I was struck with the idea of decorating my new kitchen in apples as a happy reminder of my home state of Washington. Well, I bought the mugs, my roommates gave me an apple kitchen shower and now, ten years later, I have a pretty impressive collection of apples. I have dishes and baskets, a lamp and a clock, tree ornaments, frames and even a quilted wall hanging. Each piece in my collection reminds me of a special person, place or moment in time.

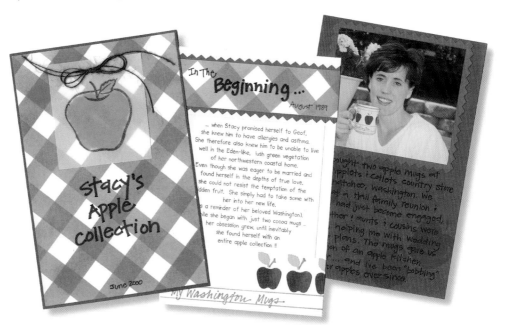

"Stacy's Apple Collection" by Stacy Julian

Album: 6" x 9" three-ring binder, Sew Be It, Timeless Tapestry

Patterned Paper: Close To My Heart

Scissors: Pinking edge, Family Treasures

Apple Stamp on Title Page: DeNami

Computer Font: Doodle Basic, "Page Printables," Cock-A-Doodle Design

Idea to Note: The apple on the cover was created by stamping on vellum, then coloring on the underside of the vellum. The vellum was then tied to the title page with red and green twine.

SEVERAL YEARS AGO I RECEIVED AN INVITATION to a party that changed my life. I was a young mother, working and struggling to make ends meet while my husband was in medical school. A friend called and invited me to a stamp party. "Postage stamps?" I asked. "No—rubber stamps," she told me, as visions of self-inking address stamps flew through my mind. Boy, was I in for a shock! After ten minutes of instruction in decorative stamping, I was hooked and I knew I had found my hobby. I clipped grocery coupons, offered to put in extra hours at work, and even considered selling my blood plasma, just so I could buy rubber stamps! I am definitely a paper crafts girl, and I now boast an entire room in my home—my stamping studio—dedicated to my passion.

I don't know if my great-grandmother had a hobby—perhaps she didn't have the free time to devote to such things. But I would love to know what creative outlets she had and what sorts of activities brought her the kind of happiness that my hobby has brought me. Creating a scrapbook dedicated to a hobby or a personal passion is a wonderful way to portray yourself. It lets others catch a little glimpse inside your soul and see just a part of what makes you unique.

Because there are as many different hobbies and passions as there are individuals, a hobby scrapbook can take many different forms. To help you explore the possibilities and get your creative juices flowing, I'll give you a few general guidelines and then highlight two albums created by friends of mine—one about a scrapbooking obsession and the other on a passion for home improvement.

"The Scrapbook of My Obsession" by Marilyn Healey

Album: 7" x 5", Generations by Hazel

Patterned Papers: Provo Craft, Northern Spy, Keeping Memories Alive, Making Memories, The Paper Patch, Karen Foster Design

Daisy Punch: Carl Mfg.

Computer Fonts: CK Anything Goes, "The Best of Creative Lettering" CD Vol. 1, *Creating Keepsakes;* Doodle Basic, "Page Printables" CD, Cock-a-Doodle Design

I don't know if
my great-grandmother
had a hobby *—perhaps*
she didn't have the free
time *to devote to such things.*

My Grandmother
Marilyn Claire Peterson Openshaw
holding my Father
Ronald Dale Openshaw
1945

My Grandmother died when my Dad was 11 years old. All pictures of the family were taken by her so because of her death there aren't many pictures of my Dad any older than 11 years old.

In 1997, the existing pictures, kept by my Grandfather, were divided up among my Dad, and his sister and brother. I took my Dad's portion of the pictures to put into an album for his birthday. I discovered that not many of the pictures had any names or dates on them. When my Grandpa came to visit I asked him to help me out, but he didn't know much about her childhood pictures, and couldn't remember much about the family ones.

I thought this was terrible. All of those memories where lost forever because my Grandmother hadn't labeled all of the pictures and now she was gone. I wasn't going to let this happen to my memories.

Why I Scrapbook

"THE SCRAPBOOK OF MY OBSESSION"

Using a little 5" x 7" post-bound album, Marilyn Healey has created a scrapbook about her love of scrapbooking. She begins with a title page and a dedication page explaining why she began creating photo albums. In her book, she's created pages about her workstation, the internet resources she uses most, and the job she has teaching scrapbooking to other devotees. Marilyn included three sections that will require occasional updates: one with samples of her favorite patterned papers, one with an index of completed layouts (also containing thumbnail photos of her award-winning and published pages) and lastly a section devoted to scrapbooking friends!

Notice how Marilyn's title and section pages all follow a similar format with ripped patterned paper placed horizontally across the bottom of the page, just above the title. Marilyn also used a flower punch as an embellishment throughout her album. She notes that as a mother of two boys, she just doesn't get to use it enough!

There are many aspects to a hobby that you can feature in your album. Think about some of these areas:

• *History.* How did you become interested in this hobby? Who introduced you to it? How long have you been involved with it and why is it something you like so much?

• *Accomplishments.* Have you been recognized in any way because of your hobby? If your hobby involves creating something, how do your early projects compare with your most recent?

• *Influences and Associations.* Do you have someone you consider a mentor or admire for their influence? Do you belong to a club or group that shares your passion? Is there a favorite store, web site or magazine that gives you inspiration and ideas regarding your hobby?

• *Time and Place.* How much time do you devote to your hobby? Do you have a regularly scheduled time or place for pursuing your hobby? Where do you go to immerse yourself in your passion?

• *Supplies.* Are there any tools, equipment or special supplies you use or have invested in for this hobby?

Decide how you want to organize your album—you might use the areas above as possible sections, or look at the two examples here for some ideas. Make sure you create a title page that includes your name, the date and the subject of your hobby. If you're dividing your album into several sections, consider creating a table of contents. Select a color scheme that "fits" your hobby. Try to use a similar design technique or page embellishment throughout your album to provide some consistency (again, the albums here provide some good examples).

Finally, make sure to include photos in your album! Have someone take pictures of you participating in various aspects of your hobby. Photograph your hobby "workplace" and supplies, people you associate with, completed projects you've created and so on. If you're still unsure as to how to get started on your album, study the two books here for some creative direction!

PAM TALLUTO SELECTED AN 8.5" X 11" TAPESTRY binder as the perfect home (no pun intended!) for pages documenting her love of interior design and her efforts in transforming a house into a home. Pam begins her book with a title page that gives a brief history of her home, introduces her decorative Americana theme, and features a contents list. In her book, she's created sections on the yard, the floor plan and the individual rooms (one page for each), including the kitchen, breakfast room, family and living room, bath and each bedroom. The dark blue cardstock Pam uses as a background for all her pages works well with her Americana theme and provides a strong sense of continuity throughout her entire book.

I love the format Pam used for each section page. "Before" and "after" photographs are mounted next to each other, and a journaling box details what was done to give the room its makeover. Behind these section pages, Pam can update her album with pages featuring fabric swatches, wallpaper samples and close-up photos of individual decorations. What fun it would be to turn to the family room section and find a list of all the board games the Tallutos love to play and who wins each game most often. The kitchen section could be spiced up by adding a few of Pam's favorite recipes, photos of Friday pizza nights and special holiday menus she prepares. Pam's album is a wonderful way to capture some of the little touches of love that have created a home where her family is sure to make lots of fond memories.

As you can see from these two albums, a hobbies and passions book can be as different as the hobby itself, as unique as the person creating the album. But no matter what form your hobby book takes on, it will be an important addition to your very own personal history.

"My Home Improvement Book" by Pam Talluto

Album: Country Home Tapestry, Hiller

Patterned Paper: Paper Patch (striped)

Computer Font: Doodle Tipsy, Cock-a-Doodle Design

Star and Heart Punches: Marvy Uchida

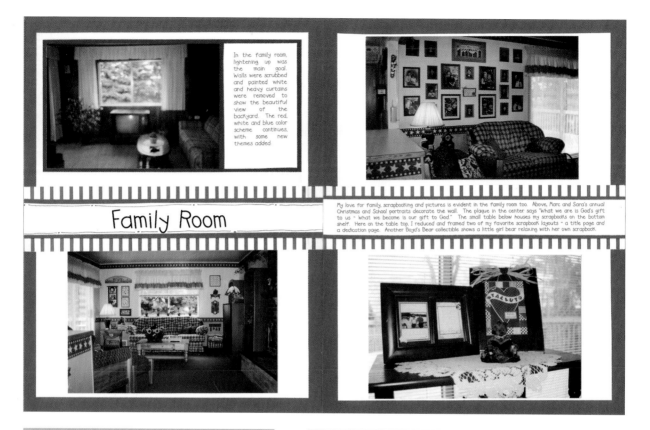

In the family room, lightening up was the main goal. Walls were scrubbed and painted white and heavy curtains were removed to show the beautiful view of the backyard. The red, white and blue color scheme continues, with some new themes added.

Family Room

My love for family, scrapbooking and pictures is evident in the family room too. Above, Marc and Sara's annual Christmas and School portraits decorate the wall. The plaque in the center says "What we are is God's gift to us - What we become is our gift to God." The small table below houses my scrapbooks on the bottom shelf. Here on the table top, I reduced and framed two of my favorite scrapbook layouts - a title page and a dedication page. Another Boyd's Bear collectible shows a little girl bear relaxing with her own scrapbook.

PREPARATION

1 Decide what hobby you'd like to feature, and choose an appropriate size and style of album.

2 Brainstorm a bit about the aspects of your hobby you'll want to preserve. (See Guidelines, p. 42, for some suggestions.)

3 Choose two or three colors and a theme for your album. Purchase some coordinating paper or other page embellishments to use throughout your book.

The family room is one of my favorite rooms. Other than Americana, themes include game boards, bird watching and teddy bears. And of course, lots of family pictures!

On the mantel, Boyd's Bear collectibles reflect life in the Talluto family. Mom, Dad, son and daughter playing a game of checkers, and Flash McBear, of course, represents Mom's obsession with photography/scrapbooking!

The bluest skies you've ever seen are in Seattle, and the hills the greenest green in Seattle . . . . so begins a song about my hometown. Even though I've now lived more than half of my life away from Seattle, it will always be my home. I cherish my childhood memories there—even more, it seems, since I've been away. Each time I return, I take my boys on what I call "Seattle celebrations": a ferry boat ride and fish and chips at Ivars on Pier 54; a trip to the Ballard locks to see if any fish are swimming up the ladder; feeding ducks at Log Boom Park and watching the sea planes land at the Kenmore Air Harbor. As we do these things together, I talk about what it was like when I was young and how things have changed. The drive-in theater where I saw "Jaws" is now a Park-n-Ride, the "brand new" playground equipment at my grade school is ancient-looking, and the discount store where I made so many great purchases is all boarded up. But there's one thing I know will never change about my beloved city—the rain! So I've created a quick and easy book all about Seattle and how in my mind it will always REIGN!

Creating a hometown album is a wonderful way to not only pay tribute to the town of your youth, but also to record some of your memories spent there. Your finished book will also be a fun way to teach your family a little about the place you spent so much time in growing up—especially if they haven't had the chance to visit themselves.

If you consider yourself to have several hometowns, you can still create a hometown book. See p. 48 for a variation.

"Seattle Reigns" by Stacy Julian

Album: 8.5" x 11", Sew Be It, Timeless Tapestry

Patterned paper: Seattle papers, Lasting Memories; Green plaid, Unknown

Die Cuts: Space Needle, Lasting Memories; All others, Ellison

Idea to Note: The photo on the left side of the tree spread (p. 46) is a color copy of a 1968 photo.

Stacy used photo transfer paper to transfer a photo of Seattle to the front of the fabric-covered album.

The main focus of this album is a list of the top ten things you love about your home state, city or town. Your list of favorites might include such things as places with special memories, local landmarks, parks, the flora and fauna, annual events, a sports team, activities such as biking or shopping, the weather or everyday buildings like the school, church, or library.

To begin your album, create a two-page title spread. On the right page, mount a postcard of your city or town. On the left page, include your list of ten favorite things, along with a title that indicates the name of your city or town. As you decorate the page, try to include colors or embellishments that reflect a little bit of the personality of the city. (For example, I found a die cut of the Seattle Space Needle to use on mine.) This title spread also becomes your table of contents!

Next, make simple two-page spreads for each item on your list. Here, you can include photographs (past and present) featuring that place or item, as well as journaling that explains why you chose that item for your "Top Ten" list. To give your ten different spreads a feeling that they belong together, repeat an element or color from your title page on each one. In my album, I created a title box on each layout spread using the same blue cardstock, pen and handwritten font as my title page. Then, you can focus the rest of your page design on highlighting the specific list item.

Finally, create a map page where you can mark the location of

I cherish

my childhood

memories *there*

even more, it seems,

since I've been away.

1   Purchase a postcard of your home state, city or town.

2   Make a list of ten things you love about your hometown (see Guidelines, p. 46, for some suggestions).

3   Start taking pictures of the items on your list, or look through your past photos to find some featuring those items.

4   Select several die cuts, stickers or other embellishments you can use throughout your book to help you highlight the things on your list.

5   Purchase a map of your city or make a color copy of one from a road atlas.

6   Select and purchase an album if needed. I chose to use an 8.5" x 11" post-bound album, but this project would work well with almost any size.

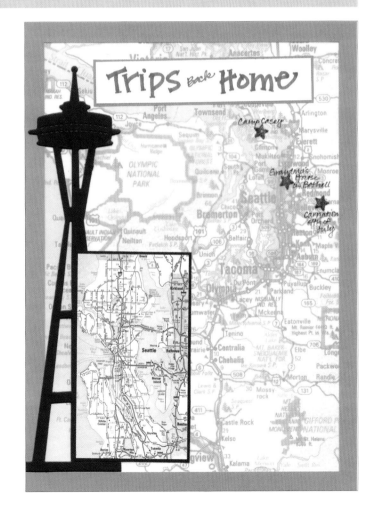

the different areas mentioned in your favorites list. I didn't want to mark directly on the map, so I used a separate piece of vellum (framed in blue cardstock) on which I placed stars and wrote the names of each location. The vellum sheet can then be laid directly over the map or even stored in a separate sheet protector.

You can also use your map page as a title page for a "Trips Back Home" section in your album, like I did. In this section, include photos and pages about the things you see and do on each visit back to your hometown. I decided to simply use divided photo pages, so all I need to do is slip the photos of our trips in place without having to worry about creating entire page layouts.

FUN IDEA If you've never left your hometown, consider yourself lucky, and create a "Happenings around Here" section instead. Here, include photos from local attractions and day trips, and newspaper clippings you find interesting. This is a perfect place to display annual pictures from a local festival. Take a picture of a landmark (or even your front yard!) every few years to show how it changes. Use the map to mark where you live as well as some of the local sites you've visited.

IF YOU'VE MOVED AROUND THE COUNTRY A BIT, take a look at the great variation of this album that Jenny Jackson created. Called "Home Is Where the Heart Is," it beautifully celebrates each of the places the Jackson family has called home.

Jenny chose a heart theme for her entire book to correspond with her album title. She selected several similar heart stamps to create a fun repetitive border along the bottom of each page. After her title page, Jenny created a table of contents spread featuring a family photo and a die cut of the United States as a key to all the locations her family has lived. Each city is represented on the map by a different colored heart, which indicates the color used to decorate that city's section in the album. Her table of contents also lists each location and the dates her family lived there. (If your homes have all been within the same or neighboring states, you might want to include a smaller-scale map to make pinpointing the locations easier.)

Then, Jenny created a section for each of her family's homes, with a two-page spread beginning each section. On the left-hand side, she included the name of the city and a photo or two of the family's home. On the right-hand side, she used lined paper to add lots of journaling about the home and the area. She also included another photo and a large heart containing that home's address and phone number. The heart border along the bottom of each page was stamped in the corresponding color from the table of contents page. Using rubber stamps makes these pages come together very quickly—all Jenny had to do was use a different color ink to create a consistent look throughout her album.

Finally, Jenny created fill-in pages for each city's section featuring some of the places her family has enjoyed visiting there. With just a few photos and a list of favorite attractions, her album is easily updated and becomes a great family record.

Even if there hasn't been a song written about your hometown, you can still pay tribute to it by creating a quick, easy and fun hometown album!

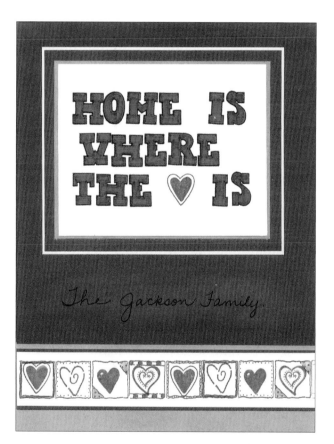

"Home Is Where the Heart Is" by Jenny Jackson

Album: 8.5" x 11" post-bound, Pioneer

Patterned Paper: Close To My Heart

Letter, Heart and Flag Stamps: Close To My Heart

Journaling Paper: Close To My Heart

♥ PROVO, UTAH (DECEMBER 1991 - JUNE 1994)
♥ ALBUQUERQUE, NEW MEXICO (JUNE 1992 - JULY 1992)
♥ EL PASO, TEXAS (JUNE 1994 - JULY 1995)
♥ SALT LAKE CITY, UTAH (JULY 1995 - JULY 1997)
♥ WASHINGTON DC (JULY 1997 - JUNE 2001)

Even if there hasn't
been a song written
about your hometown,
you can still pay **tribute**
to it by creating a quick,
easy and fun
hometown **album!**

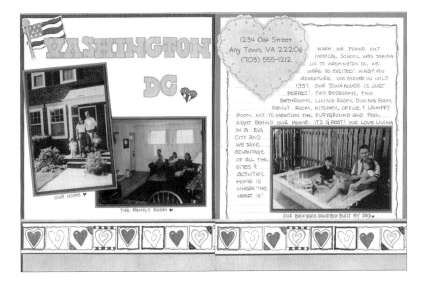

WASHINGTON DC

OUR HOME ♥

THE FAMILY ROOM ♥

1234 Oak Street
Any Town, VA 22206
(703) 555-1212

WHEN WE FOUND OUT MEDICAL SCHOOL WAS TAKING US TO WASHINGTON DC, WE WERE SO EXCITED! WHAT AN ADVENTURE. WE MOVED IN JULY 1997. OUR TOWN HOUSE IS JUST PERFECT! TWO BEDROOMS, TWO BATHROOMS, LIVING ROOM, DINING ROOM, FAMILY ROOM, KITCHEN, OFFICE & LAUNDRY ROOM, NOT TO MENTION THE PLAYGROUND AND POOL RIGHT BEHIND OUR HOME. IT'S GREAT! WE LOVE LIVING IN A BIG CITY AND WE TAKE ADVANTAGE OF ALL THE SITES & ACTIVITIES. HOME IS WHERE THE HEART IS!

OUR BACKYARD SANDBOX BUILT BY DAD ♥

AS A YOUNG GIRL, I COULD SPEND HOURS IN THE woods behind my house. There was a great big fallen tree with all of its roots exposed and near it was my special, secret spot, my place to go when I needed to get away from the world. It was the place where I retreated when I felt confused or melancholy, misunderstood or uninspired. I don't live near my special spot anymore, but I still—almost without exception—take a walk every morning. I breathe in the fresh air and allow it to clear my mind and invigorate my intellect.

I share my strong affinity for the outdoors with my father. I once asked my dad where his favorite place to visit was. He responded immediately, "the mountains." There is just something about being in nature that allows my heart and mind to combine forces in an energetic renewal of my whole soul. Hey, that's almost poetic, but really, it's true. I have often thought about compiling a scrapbook about my connection to nature, but it wasn't until I saw the beautiful little book that Sharon Soneff created that I felt truly motivated.

Sharon's nature journal is a celebration of all the aspects of nature that have held special significance for her family. We all interact with nature to one degree or another. Creating a small nature journal gives you a wonderful place to spotlight those encounters and create a strong presentation of beauty and emotion.

"Nature Journal" by Sharon Soneff

Album: 6" x 8.5" post-bound, Dalee Book Co.

Patterned Paper: Hot Off The Press (leaf paper on Table of Contents spread)

Mulberry Paper: Printworks

Handmade Paper: Craft-T

Rubber Stamps: Thistle and bee, Hero Arts; All others, Close to My Heart

Pens: Pigma Micron, Sakura

Computer font: Papyrus (used for titles and quotes)

Leaf Skeleton: Black Ink (used on title page)

Other: Natural elements like moss, twigs, flowers, etc.

Idea to Note: Sharon created a soft, subtle pattern on many of her pages with rubber stamps. Using an ink just slightly darker than the color of your paper will result in a wonderful background.

"Nature never did betray
The heart who loved her."
Wordsworth

Table of Contents

Sea and Shore
Forest and Mountain
Rock and Sand
Fur and Feathers
Flower and Leaf

NATURE JOURNAL GUIDELINES

As usual, begin by creating a title page and a table of contents for your album. You might divide your journal into sections based on the seasons (photos taken in the winter, summer, etc.); by activity, such as camping, sailing, road trips and so on; or by location, such as regions of the country, states or cities. Sharon chose to divide her book according to the different aspects of nature, such as animals, plants and flowers, and land formations. She titled her five sections: Sea and Shore; Forest and Mountain; Rock and Sand; Fur and Feathers; and Flower and Leaf.

Try to use colors and supplies throughout your book that are reflective of nature, such as earth tone colors and handmade or mulberry papers. Sharon used a torn paper technique throughout her album for photo mats and journaling blocks to contribute to the natural feel. And don't be afraid to include objects such as sand, pressed leaves and flowers, sticks and raffia. (Just make sure that the

item is protected, if needed, and doesn't come in direct contact with photographs.)

Next, create a subtitle page for each section. Sharon followed a similar format for each of her subtitle pages by mounting a related quote on the top half, then tearing the section's title in an oval shape on the bottom half and including one or two simple natural decorative elements, such as feathers.

The fill-in pages for each section can be added with time. Sharon's pages feature one or two photographs, a small torn title, another quote and some handwritten, descriptive journaling—the most important element! If you're not sure what journaling to include, spend a few minutes looking at each picture, letting your mind wander back to the time it was taken. Jot down a few notes—not so much dates and names of places, but feelings. Use lots of adjectives and describe sights, sounds, smells and textures that come to mind about the photo. Ask people who were with you what they remember. Your journaling doesn't necessarily have to focus solely on what's featured in the picture. Instead, your memories might relate more to what you were doing just before or after the photo was taken. And don't worry if you're not a naturalist who can accurately name the species of every animal, flower or plant pictured. What's important is recording your

Sharon's nature journal is a celebration *of all the aspects of nature that have held* special *significance for her family*

thoughts and feelings about the beauty of nature and your encounter with it. You can always add the Latin names later!

FUN IDEA To give your album a more serene—even reverent—tone, choose some nature-related poetry, quotes or scriptural verses to include throughout your pages, as Sharon did. There are many books available with nature quotations, and you can also find lots of quotes by doing a quick search on the internet.

Just think, if I had a photograph and some written feelings from just a few of the times my dad has been to the mountains, what a treasure that would be! I can't wait to get started on my own family's journal and capture some of our love for nature.

"Nature is but a name
for an effect
whose cause is God."
William Cowper

Marvelous Starfish

We discovered this healthy specimen of a starfish in the rich tide pools of Pfieffer Beach in Big Sur. We were having a lovely family picnic that day at this secluded beach, & I remember vividly Jon being undaunted by the cold waters of Northern Calif. and the towering rocks. Tori had a grand time jumping & splashing in the warmer inlets of water. Summer 1993

"Always be kind to animals,
Morning, noon & night:
For animals have feelings too,
And furthermore, they bite."
John Gardner

Raccoon Encounter

This raccoon approached Gerry, Jon & I at a rest stop along highway one just outside of Big Sur. Undoubtedly hoping for food, this raccoon came up empty-handed (or should I say, "empty-paw-ed") Initially, I remember thinking how cute it was & then was struck by the fact that this indeed was a wild animal. Summer 1993

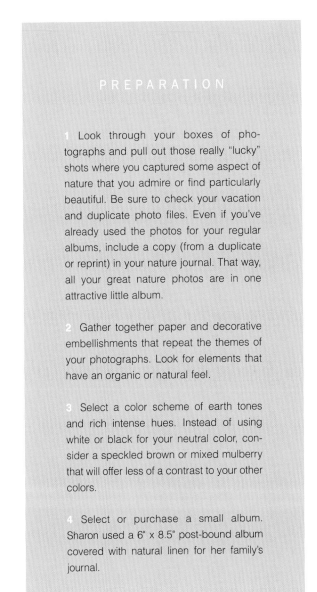

PREPARATION

1 Look through your boxes of photographs and pull out those really "lucky" shots where you captured some aspect of nature that you admire or find particularly beautiful. Be sure to check your vacation and duplicate photo files. Even if you've already used the photos for your regular albums, include a copy (from a duplicate or reprint) in your nature journal. That way, all your great nature photos are in one attractive little album.

2 Gather together paper and decorative embellishments that repeat the themes of your photographs. Look for elements that have an organic or natural feel.

3 Select a color scheme of earth tones and rich intense hues. Instead of using white or black for your neutral color, consider a speckled brown or mixed mulberry that will offer less of a contrast to your other colors.

4 Select or purchase a small album. Sharon used a 6" x 8.5" post-bound album covered with natural linen for her family's journal.

Chapter 2

Scrapbooks for Family

I think it's only natural as a parent to want to preserve some record of your family—but talk about overwhelming! In this chapter you'll find ideas to help simplify the process of scrapbooking every aspect of your family life, from creating a family history overview centered around the seasons to capturing the magic of your special relationships. If you're a new scrapbooker, why not start out by preserving just a handful of those pictures you absolutely love!

The obstacle of organization is a big one. Knowing how to sort, file and catalog memories can be quite mind-boggling. Chin up, I'm going to introduce you to two great concepts— "Family Storybook" and "Random Memories"—that will give you permission to work in a whole new way. When you can visualize your end result and have a format to follow, you can focus your enthusiasm on the creative aspects of an album.

After all is said and done, it's our family relationships and together time we cherish most. When we can capture them in a scrapbook, we have the true heart and essence of a family. We preserve the ways we are "all wrapped up in one another!"

someone in your family? "I can't wait until spring when I'm going to _____!" "Mom, in the summer can we please _____?" "Just wait honey, come fall, I'll have time to _____." "I love winter! Remember last year, we all _____?"

Piece of cake, right? So many of our family activities and memories center around the seasons of the year that some things are almost as predictable as the change in seasons themselves. These seasonal family activities wonderfully capture the overall essence of life in your home, so why not compile them in a "Scrapbook of the Seasons?" Displaying this beautiful scrapbook is an inviting and non-threatening way to share your family with friends and visitors. (I picture a big, gorgeous, coffee-table album just waiting to be picked up!)

My friend Deanna Lambson has a gift for savoring those simple joys and fleeting moments that make life worth living. Even though she's a very busy mother of four boys, I knew she would be the perfect person to ask to create a seasonal scrapbook. I gave her a short list of criteria for her book: it had to be a family album that followed a consistent format, could be easily updated and was beautiful enough to display.

Lucky for you, she agreed—and the outcome is indeed stunning! During the process, Deanna realized that if this were to be the only album she ever created, it would indeed capture the spirit of her family and summarize the most important aspects of their life together. If you've been wanting to scrapbook but didn't know where to start, this is a great project for you! Even if you have twenty or thirty years worth of photographs, simply select the best and display them in the "seasons" of your life.

"Our Book of Seasons" by Deanna Lambson

Album: 12" x 12" post-bound, Close to My Heart

Corrugated Paper: DMD Industries

Pressed Flowers: Nature's Pressed

Patterned Paper: Lasting Impressions

Photo Corners: Canson

Computer Fonts: CK Anything Goes, CK Script, and CK Print, "The Best of Creative Lettering" CD Vol. 1, Creating Keepsakes; CK Cursive and CK Wedding, "The Best of Creative Lettering" CD Vol. 2, Creating Keepsakes

Leaf Stickers: Autumn subtitle, "Celebration," Frances Meyer; Autumn "Colors" and "Traditions," Provo Craft

Butterflies: cut out from patterned paper by Provo Craft

Colored Pencils: Memory Pencils, EK Success

Mulberry Paper: Print Works

Idea to Note: Deanna created the window frames on each subtitle page by cutting strips of corrugated paper and "mitering" the corners (intersecting at 45 degree angles) to give the appearance of a wood frame.

SCRAPBOOK OF THE SEASONS GUIDELINES

A scrapbook of the seasons is naturally divided into four main sections—one for each season of the year. To give your album some consistency, create sub-sections or topics that appear under each season. Deanna chose four topics for each season: Colors, Traditions, Celebrations and People. You might use these same topics, or you might come up with your own topics based on your family's memories and photos. As you list those things that are special to your family in each season, try to use your memories first—not your photos (see the "Preparation" section).

Start by creating a title page for your album. Include an album title and any other information you wish, such as your family's name, a favorite quote or a brief description of the album's purpose. You might want to also list or visually represent each of the four main seasons. Deanna chose four seasonal photos—two featuring people and two featuring flowers—and arranged them in a window-frame setting. Or, you might take a photo of your home or a favorite deciduous tree in your yard during the height of each season and mount those four photos next to each other. Arrange the seasons in any order you want—perhaps the "traditional" order starting with spring, or perhaps starting with the season of your anniversary, since that's when your family began.

Next, create a subtitle page for each of the four seasons. Include the name of the season, a favorite seasonal

Deanna realized that if this were to be the only album she ever created, it would indeed capture *the* spirit *of her family and summarize the most important aspects of their* lives *together.*

photo and any other introductory information you want, such as a quote. You might also list the sub-topics that will appear in that section, such as "The Colors," "The Celebrations" and so on. This page will serve as an introduction to the main colors, textures and enhancements you'll use to decorate the pages within that season. Deanna tied each subtitle page back to her main title page by creating a "window frame" over a beautiful scenic photo representative of the season.

Now it's time to fill in your album! For each season, create at least one two-page spread about each topic. (You can always update your album with additional pages later.) Remember to focus less on the dates of photos and mounting them in order and more on combining photos, colors and embellishments to re-create the mood of the season. Placing photos from different generations on the same page will help strengthen your

message. Be sure to include journaling that describes some of your family's memories and activities associated with the photos.

Here's a brief description of what you might include in each section:

• Colors. This section is perfect to include at the beginning of each season. This is where you feature your best, most vibrant photographs that visually describe the season. We're going for emotion here!

• Traditions. Choose one or two photos that represent the traditions your family shares each season. Think not only of the things you do, but also the places you go and the foods you eat.

• Celebrations. What special days or holidays does your family look forward to each season? Use photos and memorabilia to present the magic of these occasions.

• People. Are there members of your family that were born in this season? Create a photo collage that pays tribute to each person and their unique personality.

Within each season, use the same colors and similar embellishments to tie the sub-topic pages together. For example, Deanna used rich fall colors of sage green, oatmeal brown, cranberry red, pumpkin and gold for all of her autumn pages, along with leaf stickers scattered throughout. In addition, try to use a similar layout or design technique throughout all the seasons to provide some consistency. For example, Deanna placed ripped strips of corrugated or patterned paper vertically along the outside edges of most of her spreads. On pages without the vertical strip, she used the same textured or patterned paper prominently behind one photo on each side. This lends a very comfortable consistency to her entire album.

Once you've created the initial spreads for each season, you can update your book as needed. Consider adding one or two photos each year—just as the season ends and your memories of the details are fresh. Using the same format for each page makes your updates quick and easy!

FUN IDEA If you'd like to include even more photos every year, you might want to use four separate albums and create a family seasonal library.

Wouldn't you just love to visit a friend, sit down and browse through a beautiful family "Scrapbook of the Seasons" like Deanna's? This album is a perfect, simple way to capture what your family is like year-round. It's a wonderful way to share your family with others and preserve a little of your family's history at the same time.

PREPARATION

1 Start by making four lists—one for each season. Write down everything that means winter, spring, summer and autumn in your family. Think of your memories first, before you look through your photos! These lists can help you determine the categories and topics to include in your album.

2 Choose two or three colors and an enhancement (such as leaf stickers for autumn) to use in the design of each season's section.

3 Select and purchase an album, if needed. Deanna chose a 12" x 12" post-bound album that allows a lot of room for photographs and journaling.

4 Begin gathering photos and memorabilia and file them according to the season and topic. Have fun viewing your photos through "sensory" eyes—focusing on sights, sounds and smells rather than the events. Look for photos that portray the essence of each season to you.

Random Memories Album

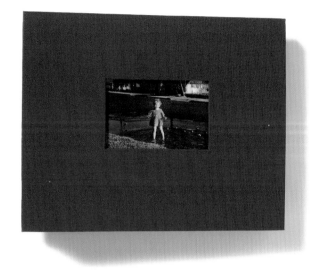

FOR A LONG TIME NOW I'VE WANTED TO CREATE a scrapbook about my life. I've spent countless hours preserving my children's memories, but the story I am best prepared to tell—and most responsible for as well—is my own. My childhood scrapbook has completely fallen apart—the pages are brown, the binding is loose and many of the photos and memorabilia have yellowed. My mom did the best she could, but it just hasn't stood the test of time. I've long contemplated how to best recompile these memories in a warm and interesting way.

One day while browsing at my local bookstore, the book *14,000 Things to Be Happy About* caught my eye. Picking it up, I found that it simply contained one long list of words that would likely bring recollections of happiness to anyone's mind. I loved it! It was the last piece of inspiration I needed. I decided to compile my own list of happy words, photos and random memories in a book I call "2000 Happy Memories."

"2000 Happy Memories" by Stacy Julian

Album: 11" x 14" post-bound with red fabric cover, Kolo

Stamps: Close to My Heart (large apple); Stampin' Up (leaf and small apple)

Punches: Marvy Uchida (apple); Family Treasures (leaf)

Patterned Paper: Colors By Design

Computer Fonts: CK Script, "The Best of Creative Lettering" CD Vol. 1, *Creating Keepsakes;* CK Journaling, "The Best of Creative Lettering" CD Vol. 2, *Creating Keepsakes*

White Opaque Pen: Hybrid Gel Roller, Pentel

This format allows you to get right to the task of writing out your priceless memories *of* people, *places,* **experiences** *and other random things.*

WHY RANDOM MEMORIES?

Creating a random memories album resolved two major scrapbooking frustrations for me. First, I have relatively few photos of my childhood. If my mom had her camera with her, she generally took only one or two pictures at an event, so it would be very difficult for me to create entire "themed" layouts that accurately captured my early history. I have also found that I often recall childhood memories as I browse through more current photos. With a random memories album, I am able to "mix it up" a little and combine the limited photos of my youth with more recent photos.

Second, my mind doesn't store and recall memories in chronological order. Rather than focus on dates and years, I focus on moments and events. If I wanted to become better acquainted with you, I wouldn't say, "So, tell me all about 1973." Instead, I'd ask you to tell me about your siblings or your favorite summer activities. A random memories album allows me to preserve my memories as I would recall them—as individual memories and stories that are interconnected and often strangely related—in a random fashion.

I think perhaps the best way to share my vision and enthusiasm for this project is to let you read a portion of the letter I've written to my boys, which I keep

tucked behind a photo on the title page of my album. I share part of it with you in the hope that it will inspire you to write something similar for your children (your letter, of course, will be as personal for you and your family as mine is for me). For all the scrapbooking we do, I wonder if our children really know what is in our hearts. It's not always easy to write a heart-to-heart letter. Most of the time, I have to sit at the computer and wait and wait for the words to come. I know, however, that having a few such letters will someday be far more priceless to our children than an entire album of decorative layouts.

> *No matter how fast life changes around you, some things will remain the same—you will always be my boys and I will always love you. You will always be able to choose to remember the happy and uplifting moments of your life and in a like manner choose not to dwell on those times that are sad, unfair, painful or discouraging. . . .*

> *About the time I decided to marry your Dad, I found some hot cocoa mugs with apples on them. Apples remind me of my childhood and youth, growing up in Washington State. I knew I wanted to buy those mugs and collect other things with apples, and display them all around me to help me remember happy times. When you grow up and have children of your own, I hope apples will remind you of me and all the good memories we have shared together. . . .*

> *When I look at this little picture of me, holding an apple, I think I was really holding my future, and because of so many good deeds and decisions that my parents and their parents and*

their parents had made . . . my future was and still is very bright. I have benefitted immeasurably by the good "seeds" that have been planted all around me. I hope you will learn of and enjoy my happy memories, plant them in your hearts and see how they grow into more happiness for you.

RANDOM MEMORIES ALBUM GUIDELINES

While "random" is a key word for this album, it is not an album without order. A random memories album follows a very specific format. A larger-sized album works best, so you have lots of room on each page for photos and text (my album is 11" x 14").

Begin your album by creating a title page that introduces the album and gives some of your reasons for creating it. You might also include a favorite photo or two, and perhaps a memory-related quote. (I'm a lover of quotes and have placed several throughout my album.) I titled my album "2000 Happy Memories" since I began creating it in the year 2000 (and hence the "2000" photo of my boys). I also included my favorite childhood photograph, which I briefly explained in the journaling below the photo and further explained in my dedication letter to my children. The letter itself is tucked behind the photo of my boys. The letter and journaling on the page also introduce and explain the apple enhancement that I used throughout the album.

Now you're ready to start adding your memories! Each two-page spread following the title page follows the same format and features 50 random memories. (In my album, these are all black pages.) On the left-hand side, list 25 happy memory words or phrases from your master list (see the "Preparation" section). Fill up the rest of the spread with 25 small- to medium-sized photos, which have been cropped and resized to fit together. (If your album has smaller pages, you might not be able to fit 50 memories on each spread.) Write a short title or caption next to each photo. One of the best things about this album is that it doesn't matter what order the photos are arranged in! This makes it easy to select photos that will fit together on a page.

Because the photos need to be cropped quite a bit to fit, I recommend using color copies or duplicate photos for this project. (You should always avoid cutting original, one-of-a-kind photos.)

Next, select a few words and photos on each spread to "highlight" with some small enhancement. I chose about 10 items per spread and used an apple punch to tie in with my cover photo and letter. For each highlighted item, write down in further detail the memory associated with it. Compile all of your written entries in an index at the back of the album. I placed my index on white pages, in alphabetical order according to the word or photo title, so the memory is easy to look up. If you can, type your index on a computer, so it can be easily updated as you add memories later on.

Eventually, you might want to create an index entry for each of your memories. I chose to start by elaborating on just a few memories for each page, and then writing about additional memories as time allowed. This lets me get all of my happy memories recorded in some form and feel like I have a "complete" album, yet still be able to easily add more information later.

FUN IDEA A random memories album is a great solution if you have several unrelated heritage photos. Simply mount each photo in an album without worrying about putting them in date order. Give each photo a title and then as you meet with family members who have information or memories about a particular photograph, simply record it and enter it in your index! While you are collecting the information over time, the photographs are kept safe in an album.

Continue creating spreads and adding to your index as you have the time and motivation. You've probably figured out that my album doesn't really contain 2000 memories. I thought I would start by completing five spreads, giving me a total of only 250 actual words and photos. I can then add a spread every so often, when I feel the urge!

FUN IDEA If I were to ever record an oral history of my life, this album would be a wonderful springboard. I could simply state the album page and photo title or word memory and then begin speaking—telling whatever story or

memory comes to mind. (Of course, you'd want to start with those memories that haven't already been highlighted in your index.)

Once in place, the random memory album format requires little creative energy yet maintains a design that is still visually sound. More importantly, this format allows you to get right to the task of writing out the priceless memories you have of people, places, experiences, stories and other random things that trigger a memory for you that might otherwise be lost to the next generation.

I LOVE THIS PICTURE OF MY HUSBAND GEOF and my grandmother. Grandma Hall is one of the most giving people I know—she is always looking for ways to uplift and help others. I'm fortunate that I married a man who is just as eager to do the same. Ever since my husband started medical school, friends and family have been seeking his "professional" advice. It doesn't matter who's calling or what time of day or night it is, Dr. Geof always says, "Sure, let's take a look." Every time I look at this picture, my heart fills with gratitude for the unselfish example of these two wonderful people in my life. They are very much alike—I guess you could say they see "eye to eye!"

I'll bet you also have a picture or two that you love. You know the kind. As you're busy organizing your photos, flipping through them at the speed of light and sorting them into piles for later use, something suddenly stops you dead in your tracks. You hear yourself say "Ohhh" as you are unexpectedly caught up in a flood of emotion. What happened? You came across a picture you love. A picture that for some reason overpowered your dedication to the task at hand and set you straight to reminiscing. A picture with a story to tell—and you are probably the best person to tell it. Put this picture and others like it in their own pile. Along with stacks of photos for your son's birthday party and last month's camping trip, you'll now have a stack labeled "Pictures I Love."

My one wish as a scrapbook instructor is for you to take a few days out of your busy schedule and start a "Pictures I Love" album. In it you will share random glimpses of yourself—your thoughts, your wishes, your memories. Imagine having such a collection of insights into your mother's or grandmother's life and soul. This type of book is at the heart of what scrapbooking is all about. Please do it!

"My Favorite Photos" by Jeannie Ferderber

Album: Vineyard Mini Photo Album (5.25" x 7.25"), Kolo

Punches: Family Treasures

Computer Font: CK Journaling, "The Best of Creative Lettering" CD Vol. 2, *Creating Keepsakes*

"The Gangs All Here"

I love these photos of the kids goofing off with each other. I look at them and just count my many blessings of all the joy and laughter they have brought into my life. October 1999

PICTURES I LOVE GUIDELINES

A "Pictures I Love" book is perfect for a small album, since you're only featuring one photo per page. Begin by creating a simple title page or by decorating the album cover. Include a title, the date you created the album and a brief description of the purpose of the book. (If you decorate the cover, you might want to include the book's introduction on the inside front cover.) My friend Jeannie Ferderber used a darling 5" x 7" album for her book, which she titled "My Favorite Photos." She used bright, fun colors and simple punched designs throughout her book—inspired by the small cover photo.

In your album, create a two-page spread for each of your favorite photos. Mount the photo all by itself on one side. If you have a group of related photos and can't choose just one as your favorite, you can include several, as Jeannie did with some pictures of her kids playing together on the floor. Add a simple enhancement or two if you want, but keep the main focus on your photo.

Then, on the other side of the spread, write about the photo. Use your own handwriting if you can—it's an important part of who you are and is a perfect addition to your words. You might want to jot down some notes on a separate piece of paper first. Think about what it is that makes you stop and go "Ohhh" as you look at this photo. Don't rush. Be patient and wait for something

"4th of July"

It's amazing how many different emotions one picture can evoke. For example, gratitude not only for the holiday being celebrated but also for the sacrifices made by many to insure our country's continuing freedom. Joy because of the four beautiful blessings pictured in the photo. Appreciation for the thoughtfulness of a friend who sent me all the matching T-shirts. And amazement that everyone was looking at the camera at the same time. July 1999

"Smooch"

Chelsea couldn't resist the chance to get up-close and personal with Uncle Floyd's cows. It was her first experience on a farm, but it didn't take her long to warm up. After feeding the cows a little straw she decided to lean forward and give one a kiss. Much to our amazement and no doubt hers too, they all decided to lean forward and return the favor. I was thrilled to actually get it on film. April 1993

to come. Don't settle for surface stuff like simply describing what is shown. Go for something deeper. How do you identify with this particular photograph? What would your grandchildren want to know?

Also, if looking at the photo in front of you causes you to recall a different time and place than the one pictured, write about it instead! Your journaling doesn't have to focus solely on the events in the photo.

FUN IDEA You can create your own "Pictures I Love" library by compiling one small album each year. Throughout the year, set aside your favorite photos in a special file. At the end of the year, narrow down your photos to a predetermined number (I've chosen fifteen) and create your "Pictures I Love" pages. You might place each year's photos in a section of a larger album (with a subtitle page introducing each year), or use separate albums for each year. Kolo makes a storage box that comes with several little booklets (like the one Jeannie used), each holding about eight photos. This set is perfect for a "Pictures I Love" library. Simply choose enough photos each year to fill one booklet. Every few years you'll add one storage box to your collection!

Whether you're a scrapbook beginner or a seasoned pro, take some time to create a small "Pictures I Love" album. This wonderful little book will be one of the most important and rewarding projects you ever do!

PREPARATION

1 Select 5, 10 or even 20 of your most favorite photos—perhaps some of your children and family, a few from your own youth, and even one or two of daisies or a sunset. The point is to "mix it up" a little. Remember, the reason these pictures belong together is not because of their date or event, but because of the feelings they inspire.

2 Purchase a small album. Jeannie used a 5.25" x 7.25" Kolo mini photo album, which is perfect for 4" x 6" photos. I used an album that holds half-sized cardstock (5.5" x 8.5").

MY OWN "PICTURES I LOVE" ALBUM FEATURES
photos from a wide time period—spanning my childhood and including recent photos of my children. In fact, many of my children's photos spark memories of my own youth. For example, when I look at a photo of my son Chase all wrapped up in a towel after swimming, I think of the countless hours I spent as a young girl swimming in an unheated backyard pool. I would swim until my teeth started chattering and my mom would make me get out and wrap me up in a towel until I was warm. Now I'm the one doing the "warming up" with my son and I love it!

I used bright colors and fun enhancements throughout my album. Using sticker letters for the titles and pre-made cut-outs let me put the pages together in a snap and spend my time focusing on the important stuff of writing down my memories. This little album is the perfect place for me to share those personal insights and memories with my children that might otherwise get left out of my scrapbooks.

"Pictures I Love" by Stacy Julian

Album: 6" x 9" three-ring binder, Wilson Jones

Patterned Paper: Lasting Impressions

Sticker Letters: Provo Craft

Pens: Zig Millennium, EK Success

Doll and Fish: Friends collection, My Mind's Eye

Daisy Punch: Family Treasures

Idea to Note: Stacy laminated the cover collage with a Xyron machine.

I HAVE A CONFESSION TO MAKE—I STARTED scrapbooking before I really had a plan. I didn't know how many books I wanted to do. One for each child? A huge volume for the entire family? A Christmas theme book? When I did create pages, I didn't really work in chronological order, either. I just loved to make layouts, so I would work on whichever group of photos caught my creative fancy.

I found myself frequently frustrated by the gaps that existed as I looked through my finished pages. Some years there were mainly layouts of major celebrations like holidays and birthdays, while other years the layouts seemed to focus more on everyday life. I wanted to be able to organize it all and feel like all my layouts belonged together. In addition, I wanted a way to encourage my children to look at all these pages I'd created for them.

My solution was slow in coming, but it's one that I absolutely love! I've written a fun family story that contains references to my completed pages as it briefly tells my family's history. My scrapbook pages, in turn, are stored and organized in my family library albums. This "family storybook" concept is quite different from organizing albums chronologically, but it has worked wonderfully well for me. It's a way to organize the layouts you've already created so you can enjoy them more easily, as well as a way to set up and categorize the new layouts you create, especially if you're a new scrapbooker. My hope is that you will be able to adapt my system to fit your own situation as you create your own family storybook!

"Family Storybook" and "Family Fun Library" by Stacy Julian

Family Library Colored Albums: 8.5" x 11" three-ring albums, Century *Family Storybook Small Notebook:* 5.5" x 8.5" three-ring album, Hiller *Computer Fonts:* PC Hugware, Color Me Kids, Provo Craft; Doodle Basic, "Page Printables" CD, Cock-a-Doodle Design; CK Script, "The Best of Creative Lettering" CD Vol. 1, *Creating Keepsakes*; CK Chunky, "The Best of Creative Lettering" CD Vol. 2, *Creating Keepsakes Other:* Clear index tabs for sub-category title pages are from Z-International, Inc. (available at office supply stores)

I wanted to be able to **organize** *it all and feel like all my layouts belonged together. In addition, I wanted to* **encourage** *my* children *to look at all these pages I'd created* for them.

FAMILY STORYBOOK AND LIBRARY OVERVIEW

Here's a brief overview of how my system works. First, you create a family storybook that tells your immediate family's story and history. I've written mine as a rebus-style story with little icons representing each family member. The storybook provides the chronology part of your family history and serves as an index to your completed scrapbook pages, which are stored in your family library albums. Small icons and colored text throughout the story become "links" that direct you to a specific album and layout in your family library. (Think of your story as your family's home page on the internet and the icons and colored text as the hyperlinks that take you to another page somewhere else.)

The family library is where all of your page layouts are organized into different albums and categories. My library (which I've called "The Family Fun Library") has four different-colored albums, one for each major category, such as "The People We Love" and "The Places We Go." Each album is then divided into sub-categories, such as "Grandparents" and "Far Away Visits." The color of the linked text in the story matches the color of the associated album and the story icons tell you which sub-section to turn to. Rather than organizing your page layouts chronologically in the library albums, they're stored according to the category in which they best fit.

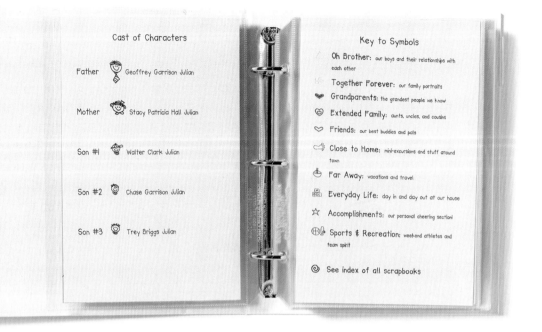

This system makes your finished pages more accessible and enjoyable by your family. A scrapbook isn't meaningful unless it's looked at and cherished, and that's what this system has helped me accomplish. Picture me calling my boys together for story time, where we read one or two chapters of our family story. I then let each child choose a "link" from the story which refers us to a section of our Family Fun Library. We look up the associated layout and discuss it. For example, if the link for Dad's medical school graduation was chosen (seen in the story as "graduated magna cum laude" in blue text, next to a special icon), we would go to the "Accomplishments" sub-catagory of our "The Things We Do" blue album, where we would find a layout about Dad's graduation. What's really neat is that we would also find pages about other family accomplishments—from Clark learning to ride a bike, to Trey's first steps, to mom writing a book! (Not every layout in your library albums will have a direct reference in your family story. Instead, each "linked" major event will refer you to a category section featuring lots of other related pages.)

Another benefit to this system is that it mixes up your "early" pages with your more current ones. Most scrapbookers improve their page design and style as they create more and more layouts, and they often think their earlier pages are less attractive. Mixing up your pages—rather than having them in chronological order—averages out the overall presentation and doesn't give you the option of not sharing those earlier pages with your family!

FAMILY STORYBOOK GUIDELINES

To create a family storybook, follow these guidelines. Start by sitting down and writing your family's story. Use a computer if you can for easy and frequent

updates. The story should deal only with the major events and dates in your family's history. Divide your story into chapters so it can be easily read in smaller pieces. Don't try to write something about every scrapbook layout you have—just highlight the most important events, and once in a while mention how your family's everyday life has changed. The idea is to direct people to a specific library album where they can then browse through all the related layouts.

As you write your story, create "links" to layouts in your library albums by highlighting pertinent names, words or phrases in a specific color, depending on which album they refer to. For example, in my library "The Places We Go" album is blue, so any link to that album would appear in blue text. You can color the words using your computer's font color feature (if you have a color printer), or by using a pen or highlighter. With each link you create, also include a small icon (Wing Ding font, stamp or sticker) that indicates which sub-category the associated page falls under.

Tip: If you use a Wing Ding font like I did, you can assign keystrokes for each icon in your word processor. This makes typing your story much easier. For example, if I want the symbol for Geof's face, I just press Alt-G on my keyboard!

Now, create a title page for your storybook as well as "Cast of Characters" and "Key to Symbols" pages. These pages provide references and brief descriptions

---

scared, she was mostly happy. While 🙂 was morning sick and learning what it was like to be pregnant, 🙂 was just-plain-sick of learning. He had been studying for two years just from textbooks, and was most anxious to start some hands-on application. As a result, they both began wearing big baggy pants. 🙂 started hospital rotations, and was given a white jacket and lots of pairs of green scrubs (🙂)! 🙂 , on the other hand, started shopping garage sales for maternity clothes and baby "stuff". During that same Summer, the Julian's also had a visit from 🙂's sister Chanda 🙂. What a fun time it was, showing her some famous Chicago sites 🏙.

The 1992 holiday season was a busy one.

🙂 & 🙂 traveled to New Mexico 🍴 for Thanksgiving 🙂, and Mitchell, IN 🍴 for Christmas 🙂. It was hard to believe another year was gone.

January 1993 was spent getting ready for baby 📷. On February 24 at 9:05 p.m. Walter Clark Julian 🙂, was born. Immediately, 🙂 & 🙂 had to make some major changes in their daily routine 📷. From midnight feedings, to diapers and baths … 🙂 (Clark) was a whole new experience! Luckily, Grandma Hall 💜 came to help 🙂 adjust. 🙂 was such a cute baby, long awaited and loved by all 🙂.

In May, 🙂 went to her doctor for a post–

10   11

for the symbols you've used and should go in the front of the storybook album.

If you've already created several smaller theme albums, you can also include an "Index to All Scrapbooks" page like I did. This page lists each smaller album I've created, with a thumbnail photo of its title page and a brief description of its content. To use this index, insert a special symbol in

1 Outline your family story (the major events since the beginning of your immediate family).

2 Purchase a small notebook or album to keep your story in.

3 Purchase a Wing Ding-style font for your computer or alternatively purchase several small stickers or stamps to use as the icon characters in your story.

4 Be ready and willing to mix things up a little when categorizing your finished layouts. If you are a very methodical or organized scrapper, this may drive you a little crazy. But trust me, it will be okay! The benefits in enjoyment will far outweigh your time in reorganization.

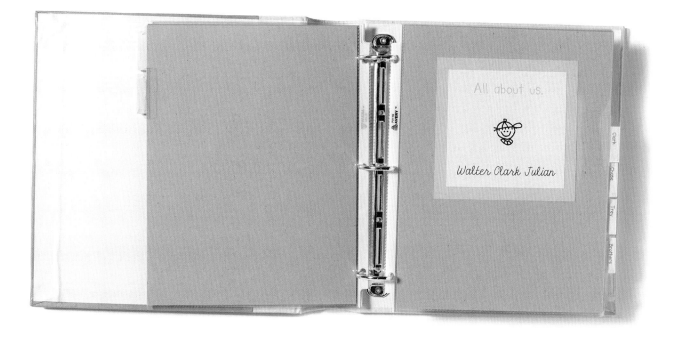

your story whenever you want to indicate that there's a special album (other than your library albums) related to that part of the story. In my story, every time you see the swirl symbol, it means that I've created another scrapbook about that particular word or phrase. For example, when I talk about how my husband and I met and married, I've included the swirl symbol (as well as highlighting the word "married" in yellow to point to the "All About Us" library album and including the icon that indicates the "Together Forever" sub-section). On the "Index to All Scrapbooks" page, you'll find a description of my romance album ("The Love of My Life") which gives much more information about our relationship. *Note:* Rather than use a unique story symbol for each of my smaller theme albums, I chose to use only one symbol that refers to the index page. This makes it easier to update the story and index, although it's not always immediately obvious which theme album is being referred to.

Finally, store your family story and index pages in their own small notebook or album.

FAMILY LIBRARY GUIDELINES

The second part of my organizational system involves setting up your family

library, where you organize your completed scrapbook pages. First, you need to determine what categories and sub-categories you want to use for your library. I chose four main categories: All About Us, The People We Love, The Places We Go, and The Things We Do. I used a separate album and a different color for each category to help make linking from the family story easier.

Then, I created sub-categories within each major category. The sub-categories should reflect the types of activities your family is involved in—and you can always add new categories if you need to! Here are my sub-categories:

1. ALL ABOUT US (YELLOW ALBUM)
   A. One section for each family member, for individual portraits and pages capturing our personalities and individual perspectives
   B. "Oh Brother" for sibling relationship pages (I have all boys)
   C. "Together Forever" for layouts of family portraits
2. THE PEOPLE WE LOVE (RED ALBUM)
   A. "Grandparents"
   B. "Extended Family"
   C. "Friends"
3. THE PLACES WE GO (GREEN ALBUM)
   A. "Far Away" for vacations and travel
   B. "Close To Home" for our homes, neighborhood sites, day trips, and so on
4. THE THINGS WE DO (BLUE ALBUM)
   A. "Everyday Life" for everything from baking cookies to visiting the dentist and all the stuff in between
   B. "Accomplishments" for our own cheering section!
   C. "Sports and Recreation" for weekend sports and the things my family does to relax and have fun

Remember that you can use whatever categories fit your family and photos. For example, I included a "Sports and Recreation" category because I have lots of these types of pages—you might want to use a "Dance and Theater" category instead. Or, you might want to create a "Holidays" category; I don't have one because I store most of my holidays pages in a separate holiday album—see Chapter Four.

Once you've decided on your categories, create a title page for each category and sub-category section. I adhered a little tab to the outside of each sub-category title page's sheet protector so it's very easy to turn to each section's beginning. Also, notice that my title pages each have a white label using the Wing Ding faces from my story. I adhered this white piece of cardstock with a removable adhesive so I can print a new one with additional faces if our family grows!

The label on the outside cover of each album is permanent, with just the title of the book (no Wing Ding faces) and the text "Volume One." This makes it easy to create additional volumes later on as the first volume fills up with layouts.

Now, you're ready to start categorizing your completed layouts! Since the library system requires you to move layouts around, it really only works if your completed layouts are in three-ring binders or post-bound albums. If your layouts can't be moved around (or you don't want to move them), see the "Family Library Variation" section for another idea.

I haven't found a layout yet that doesn't fit into one of my categories. Sometimes it's a little tricky. For example, does a page about Chase getting a haircut go into Chase's section or into the everyday life section? The great thing is, there's no wrong answer! (I chose everyday life). My categories also help me focus on the more meaningful aspects of the events I'm scrapbooking. As I'm creating a page, I ask myself if I want my page to emphasize a relationship, a place we love, a unique part of someone's personality, and so on.

Once you have your layouts categorized by subject, you can use divided sheet protectors to display additional photos or to hold photos waiting to be put on a decorative layout (see below).

IF YOU ALREADY HAVE CHRONOLOGICAL ALBUMS
and you can't or don't want to move your pages around,
consider using this adaptation to the family library system. Instead of actually moving your pages into library
categories, you might want to just categorize your layout
titles on an index page. For example, all of your pages
depicting a relationship would be listed in the index
under "The People We Love," along with the corresponding album and page number. If one of those relationship pages also features a place you love to visit, you
can include its title under "The Places We Go" as well.
The idea is to create the "big picture" and connect and
cross-reference your pages to your family story.

I cannot tell you how rewarding the storybook and
index systems have been for me! I finally feel like my
scrapbook pages are telling the whole story—and my
children are getting more out of our family's albums
than ever before. Start on your family's story today!

"The Garrod Family Scrapbook Index" by Sally Garrod

Stickers: Me & My Big Ideas

Computer Font: CK Toggle, "The Best of Creative Lettering" Vol. 2,

Creating Keepsakes

FOR TEN YEARS NOW I'VE FELT GUILTY ABOUT not having a wedding album. But for some reason I could just never seem to get started on one. Perhaps because it was such an important day and I wanted the scrapbook to be perfect. Or perhaps because I wasn't quite sure where to begin. (And there's always the theory that I'm subconsciously resisting remembering all the details because I was sick and my mother made me take a nap after the ceremony that day!) Whatever the reason, I'd grown so tired of putting it off that I committed myself to completing it for Valentine's Day as a gift for my husband. But even then, I still couldn't do it!

Finally, late one night I realized that while my wedding day was a very significant event in my life, it was just that—an event. One single day. What I truly wanted to celebrate and capture in a book was the relationship I have with this husband of mine, the love of my life. After changing my focus, I was finally able to put together an album about my wedding (whew!) and much more at the same time. My album not only has the story of our courtship, engagement and marriage, but it also has photos and memories of all our shared special times, from dates to special vacations to those unexpected trials when our relationship grew even stronger. It's also an album I can update in the years to come with additional stories and photos as we forge through life together.

Whether or not you already have your wedding album done, why not go a step further and create a little romance book to capture even more of your special memories? You can preserve some of the history, highlights and magic of the relationship with your true love.

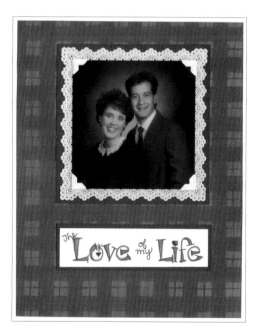

"The Love of My Life" by Stacy Julian

Album: 8" x 10", Creative Memories

Patterned Paper: Red plaid, Colors by Design

Doilies and Heart Stamps: Close To My Heart

Computer Font: CK Journaling, "The Best of Creative Lettering" CD Vol. 2, *Creating Keepsakes*

Lettering: Hearts alphabet, *The Art of Creative Lettering*, Creating Keepsakes Books

Idea to Note: The quote pages were created by printing the text on vellum paper, then adhering the vellum to a hand-stamped background with a Xyron machine.

ROMANCE BOOK GUIDELINES

A romance book can take many different forms, from serious and sentimental to light-hearted and whimsical. It doesn't matter which approach you take, as long as your book has lots of your own personality in it. Start by creating a title page that introduces the two main "characters" featured in your book, either by name, with a photo or both. Give your album a title that reflects the tone you want to set. I titled my book "The Love of My Life," while my friend Pam titled hers "Someday My Prince Will Come" (see Variation, p. 80).

Next, decide what aspects of your relationship you want to feature in your album. Consider including some of the following:

- The story of how you met and fell in love. You could do a "he says, she says" take, where you coax your husband into writing his version of the story and then add your own version (the true version, of course).
- Photos, memorabilia, and keepsakes of major events, as well as some of the everyday things you've experienced together, including any traditions you share.
- Your particular philosophy on love, or specific rules or guidelines you've tried to follow for success in your marriage and relationship.
- A list of the reasons you love each other.
- An "over the years" section highlighting photos of you as a couple.

What I truly wanted

to **celebrate**

and capture in a book

was the relationship

I have with this husband

of mine, the love

of my life.

- A page or two dedicated to the interests, hobbies and activities you share together.
- A travelogue where you briefly note the trips you've taken together, from weekend getaways to long-awaited vacations.

You might decide to organize your album into different sections, as I did. If so, create a table of contents as well as a subtitle page for each section. I came up with five sections for my book:

- Our Story: How we met and married
- Two is Better than One: Triumphs, trials and milestones
- Together Forever: Our shared philosophies on forging family life
- Our Special Times: Dates, trips, anniversaries and celebrations
- Keepsakes: Notes, cards and gifts

Notice that I didn't use a chronological organization for my album. This allows me to easily see the passage of time by arranging photos together that were taken years apart. It also lets me quickly update my book and add more information later, so I don't feel like I need to have all my photos and keepsakes gathered and in chronological order before I can begin my book.

Try to select one or two colors and a simple enhancement to use throughout your album. This makes it quick and easy to put your pages together and also adds continuity to your book. For example, in the table of contents, I used a different heart stamp to designate each section. Then, I used the same stamp as

---

Among intelligent people the surest basis for marriage is friendship – the sharing of real interests, the ability to fight out ideas together, and understand each other's thoughts and dreams.

~Kahlil Gibran
from Mary Haskell's journal
May 26, 1923

Geoffrey Garrison Julian

...was born in Lancaster, California on May 15, 1966. His family consisted of his parents, Gary Allen Julian and Valerie Clark Julian as well as his sister Amy. Geof had a happy childhood and knew from an early age he wanted to be a doctor. He grew up and went to BYU where he majored in Zoology. One of the classes he was required to take was physics. While the lectures were interesting, it was the physic's lab that Geof most enjoyed. His all time favorite experiment was ...

Stacy Patricia Hall

... was born in Pullman, Washington on May 6, 1965. She also lived with a loving and happy family. Her parents, Parley Briggs Hall and Connie McDougal Hall had two sons, Theron and Cougar and two other daughters, Darci and Chanda. Growing up, Stacy's father would remind her that when she went to BYU, she should take tough classes like chemistry and physics ... so she could meet and marry a doctor. Well ...Stacy did take physics, and it was in the lab, that she conducted her most favorite experiment ...

Distance Makes the Heart Grow Fonder ...
...or how I knew Geof was the one for me
(As told by Stacy)

In July 1988 (six months before meeting Geof), I won a trip to Germany on the radio. It's true. My Mom had asked me to run to Safeway to pick up a few things, and while on the pop aisle, I saw an advertisement for a sweepstakes called Europe's Seven Cities of Summer. I filled out several entry blanks, mailed them in and won! Now, one year later, Geof and I had been dating since February and everything seemed to be going really well. We were enjoying the relaxed atmosphere at BYU during Spring and Summer terms .. taking picnics, going on hikes, watching the stars .. love was definitely in the air! It came time for me to go home and take my long awaited trip .. we said good-bye and parted for the first time since meeting. On the long flight to Frankfurt, Mom and I did a lot of talking about Geof and I. She asked if I knew he was the one I would marry. I felt pretty sure .. but told her neither one of us wanted to rush. I suspected if everything continued to develop, we might get engaged at Christmas and married in the spring. Browsing through the in-flight magazine, I came across a picture of a wedding ring in a jewelers ad. It was really different .. a style I liked, so I ripped it out. I knew it was too soon to give the picture to Geof, so I tucked it away to give to him later. Our trip was fantastic (another scrapbook altogether) and I really enjoyed spending time with my parents one on one .. however, I missed Geof! I wanted to share everything I was seeing with him and I just couldn't get him off my mind. I had $1000 spending money and wanted to spend it all on him. I had one photo of us together that I looked at everyday day, probably every hour. I wasn't frantic .. I just didn't feel complete .. I had never had such a great desire to share every moment with someone. The Saturday after we got home, Geof was scheduled to come to Seattle on the train. We would visit with family for a few days and then drive back to the "Y" together. Well .. I couldn't wait to see him. I was really nervous, ... what if he hadn't missed me as much as I had missed him? His 5:00 p.m. arrival became 7:00 p.m. and then 10:00 p.m. and then finally 3:00 a.m.. I would have to wait until morning to see him. I was ready to walk out the door to church Sunday morning, when the phone rang! I ran, picked it up and heard his voice .. he had to see me right away! The ten minute drive seemed like an hour, but I finally pulled up in front of his parents house. He came right out and walked over and gave me the biggest hug! I knew right then .. he was the one. I felt like I had come home. It felt so right. Of course, I had no idea what Geof had in store for me!

This is the picture I carried all over Germany!

Love Waits for No Man ...
... or how I asked Stacy to marry me
(as told by Geof)

Stacy was returning to Seattle from Germany after a two week trip with her parents. I had decided to surprise her with a proposal and wedding ring when she returned. Stacy was supposed to come over on Sunday after church. I discussed with my parents the plans of my proposal. We would all go out to dinner that evening on the wharf in Kirkland and then Stacy and I would break away for the big moment.

I began to get nervous, so I called Stacy and asked her to come in the morning. She showed up at my house while my parents were on a walk. I decided such an event could not wait, and I told Stacy we should go down to the water. While driving out of the housing development, we stopped to talk to my parents. They asked where I was taking Stacy? I replied slyly, oh just down by the water. My parents were a bit perplexed, given that we had agreed to wait for the proposal until that evening. I said no. I was nervous her now, but we could still go back that evening too, and off we went.

The day was beautiful, and we picked a bench by the dock. A ship named Mammy was anchored in the water, with seagulls floating on the breeze above. I had placed the ring in a large book called "The Greatest Story Ever Told," and it was easily hidden amongst the thick pages. As we sat on the bench, I abruptly handed Stacy the book with little explanation. She stared at it for quite a while unsure what the meaning associated with such an old book was. With a little prompting from me, she opened to the page upon which the engagement ring was taped.

I jumped down onto my knee, and began in a shaky voice. "I love you and ask for your hand in marriage." " I couldn't be happy without you Stacy, and my wish is that my future happiness will come from making you happy," I said with an emotional croaking voice. She agreed and we enjoyed the afternoon together, later returning home to share our joyous news with my parents.

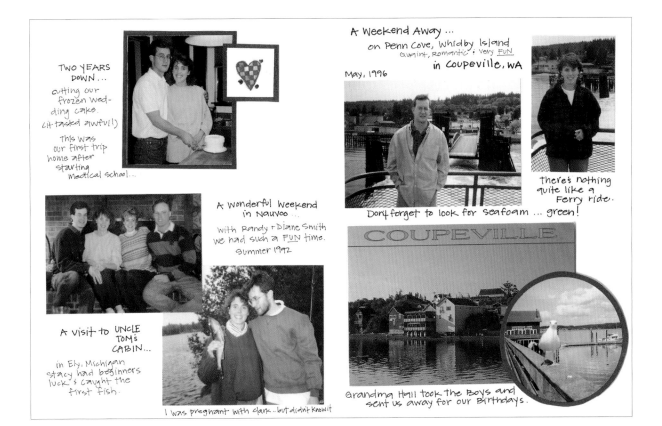

TWO YEARS DOWN...
cutting our frozen wedding cake. (it tasted awful!) This was our first trip home after starting medical school...

A Wonderful Weekend in Nauvoo...
With Randy + Diane Smith We had such a FUN time. Summer 1992

A visit to UNCLE TOM's CABIN...
in Ely, Michigan Stacy had beginners luck & caught the first fish.

I was pregnant with clark...but didn't know it

A Weekend Away...
on Penn Cove, Whidby Island Quaint, Romantic & Very FUN
in Coupeville, WA
May, 1996

there's nothing quite like a Ferry ride.

Don't forget to look for seafoam ... green!

COUPEVILLE

Grandma Hall took the Boys and sent us away for our Birthdays.

an embellishment on both the subtitle page and fill-in pages for the appropriate section.

Now, you're ready to create the main pages for your album. Create a page or two about each of the areas or sections you've chosen. Don't feel like you have to cover everything—highlight only the most important things. To help your pages come together quickly and easily, create a "decorative framework" by selecting one or two colors and a simple embellishment that matches your introductory pages. This way, you don't have to worry about decorating each individual layout. For example, on each of my fill-in pages, I simply used one or two red mats and the appropriate "section heart" (from the table of contents) as page decorations. This also lets you easily update your album in the future with additional photos.

If you want to include notes and cards in your album, you might want to create a pocket page or two. Pocket pages make your keepsakes easily accessible, and also give you a place for storing new photos and memorabilia that you want to add to your album later.

FUN IDEA Add wedding photos of your parents or other couples you admire to your romance book, along with one or two of their tips for a happy relationship.

WHEN I SHARED MY ROMANCE ALBUM CONCEPT with my friend Pam Talluto, she took the idea and ran with it, creating a fun album titled "Someday My Prince Will Come." Pam played up the "frog prince" theme by using crown patterned paper, the color green, frogs and amphibian puns throughout her book. The end result is a whimsical and inviting celebration of her real-life fairytale romance with her husband. Pam reports that this was the most fun she's ever had doing an album!

Rather than divide her book into sections, Pam used a chronological, storybook approach. This is an easy format to build on. Just start at the "Once upon a time" and tell your story to the "Happily ever after!" Pam focused more on her early romance and courtship with her husband, rather than their married years together, a perfectly fine adaptation!

FUN IDEA   Pam and her husband each created a "Top Ten" list of the things they love about one another. These lists are fun and easy—and they can reveal quite a bit about a relationship. Don't you wish you had lists like these from your grandparents?

Whether your romance book is full of red hearts and lace, fun frog princes or something totally different, it's sure to bring a smile to your spouse's face (and maybe a tear or two as well). And you might be surprised how much children enjoy learning about this more personal side of their parents. Just don't wait ten years to put it together like I did!

"Someday My Prince Will Come" by Pam Talluto

Album: 6" x 8.5", Dalee *Frog on Cover:* Little Bits by Gick

Crown Patterned Paper: Source unknown

Computer Fonts: CK Anything Goes, "The Best of Creative Lettering" CD Vol. 1, *Creating Keepsakes;* CK Toggle, "The Best of Creative Lettering" CD Vol. 2, *Creating Keepsakes*

Die Cuts: Stamping Station

Pop Dots: All Night Media

Punches: Family Treasures

Letter Stencil: ABC Tracers, Pebbles for EK Success

Stickers: Crown and Queen, Mary Engelbreit by Melissa Neufeld; Fuzzy frogs, Sandylion; Letter stickers, Provo Craft

The end result is a **whimsical** *and* *inviting* celebration *of her real-life fairytale* **romance** *with her husband.*

Relationship Flip Book

WHEN IT COMES RIGHT DOWN TO IT, THE THINGS we cherish most in our lives are often our relationships with others. I have a great relationship with my mom—we've been best friends for as long as I can remember. When we're together, we love to talk and sing songs with funny accents, go on long walks, sit and look at decorating magazines, and give each other advice on how to solve all of our problems. When I still lived at home, we'd stay up late and do silly things like blow up marshmallows in the microwave and then laugh ourselves to tears. I'll never forget the time Mom called the grade school and had the secretary announce over the loud speaker that Stacy had neglected to make her bed! (Needless to say, I haven't had a problem with bed-making since.) I could never stay mad at my mom very long—she is just way too cool.

Too often, special relationships like these get left out entirely of our scrapbooks as we focus on the events in our lives. I found a way to celebrate the relationship I have with my mom by creating a little 6" x 6" scrapbook. It's a "flip book," a quick, easy way to capture two people's perspectives on the connection they share. When I gave it to Mom, we laughed and cried all over again. Think about an extra-special relationship in your life, then sit down and create a little flip book about it before your priceless memories slip through the "scrapbook cracks!"

"A Mother, A Daughter, A Friend" by Stacy Julian

Patterned Paper: Close to My Heart

Flower Stamp: Close to My Heart (from the Awesome Blossom set)

Scissors: Pinking edge, Provo craft

Album: 6" x 6", Close to My Heart

Idea to Note: The design of each blank page seems to suggest a certain area for the journaling that will be added later. Try using striped and plaid patterns as "writing lines" in your journaling areas.

Connie McDougal Hall

HOW A FLIP BOOK WORKS

The foundation of a flip book is the comparison of two people who share a relationship. It's typically created in a small album, where half of the pages are about one person and half about the other. Identical sets of pages are given to each person containing questions about the relationship, such as "My favorite things about you are . . . " and "Remember when we used to . . . " Separately, each person writes answers and memories on one set of pages.

When the book is assembled, one person's pages are inserted normally in the album, beginning with the title page and continuing through the question pages to the middle of the book. The middle of the album contains three two-page spreads of photographs. The first spread has photos of the first person. The middle spread contains photos of the two people together. However, the right-hand side of this spread is inserted in the album upside-down. This gives your book its "flip," as the reader must then turn the book over to continue. The third spread is inserted next with photos of the second person. The book continues with the second person's pages—all upside-down and in reverse order when compared to the first half—ending with that person's title page.

If you want to create a relationship comparison book but don't like the "flip" aspect, see the variation suggestion (p. 86).

RELATIONSHIP FLIP BOOK GUIDELINES

Begin your relationship book by creating a title page for each person. Include a photograph and the person's name, and use the same page design for each page. I even went so far as to stage a "duplicate" photo for my title page by standing in a lilac bush, just like my mom was pictured. (Since lilacs are Mom's favorite flower, it was the least I could do!) The lilac photo also inspired

Stacy Hall Julian

Too often, special relationships *like these get left out entirely of our scrapbooks as we* **focus** *on the* events *in our lives.*

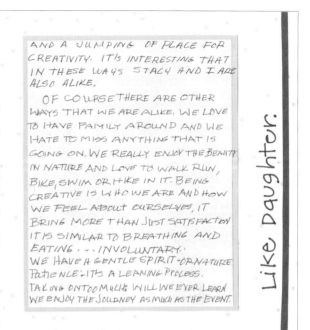

the colors and flower stamp I used as embellishments throughout the book.

Next, create a dedication spread for each person. This page introduces the relationship and includes a few photographs. My dedication pages say "A Mother, A Daughter, A Friend" and have three photos of that person, one corresponding to each aspect.

Now, you're ready for the main part of your book: the question and memory pages. Remember, you'll create two identical sets of pages. At this point, each page will be mostly blank with only the design "background," leaving room for the answers to be written in later. Try to use soft colors and simple designs as you create your pages so they won't detract from the writing and photos.

I used ten fill-in-the-blank sentences for my album. You can adapt these questions for the relationship you're highlighting (if it's not a mother/daughter album), or come up with your own.

1. "Like mother, like daughter" (list three ways we are alike).

2. "Remember when we used to . . ." (list three things we used to do).

"I loved doing these things with you because . . ." (fill in).

3. "My favorite things about you!"

(list seven to ten favorite things).

4. "My favorite family tradition is . . . " (describe a tradition).

"This tradition holds special meaning for me because . . . " (fill in).

5. "Home is the Heartland" (list a few fond memories of our home life).

6. "Spring and Summer" (list a few of the best things we did together).

"Fall and Winter" (list a few of the best things we did together).

7. "Feelings" (fill in the blanks):

"You make me laugh when . . . "

"You make me cry when . . . "

"I'm proud of you for . . ."

"I admire you for . . . "

8. "Ups and Downs:"

"When we click we both agree . . . " (list a few things we agree on).

"When we clash, we disagree . . . " (list a few things we disagree about).

9. "Unanswered Questions" (fill in the blanks):

"Why did you . . . ?"

"How did you know . . . ?"

"The best lesson I've learned from you . . . "

10. "Magic Words" (fill in the blanks).

"Please always remember . . . "

"Did I ever say thank you for . . . "

Give one set of pages to each person. Encourage each to use his or her own handwriting on the pages—it will add so much personality to the album. Also, let each person use a good, permanent, acid-free journaling marker to write their responses with.

If you want to present this album as a gift, send the other person a list of the fill-in-the-blank sentences (without the actual pages) and tell her to write out her responses. After presenting her with the book, have her transfer her responses onto the album pages. No changes allowed!

For the middle of the album, create three two-page spreads for mounting photographs—one spread each with photos of each person and one spread with photos of them together. Keep the page decoration simple—use only one or two embellishments to match the rest of your album.

Finally, assemble the pages in your album. Begin with the title and dedication pages of one person, followed by their ten question pages (in order from 1 to 10), then the spread with their photos. In the middle of the album, insert the spread of the "together" photos—only place the right-hand side of the spread upside-down to cue readers that it's time to flip. Continue with the photo spread of the second person, their question pages

(in order 10 to 1), and end with their dedication and title page. All of the second person's pages will be upside-down in comparison to the first set of pages.

FUN IDEA This project would make a great presentation at an anniversary party where both husband and wife have previously answered the questions.

PREPARATION

1   Select a small album that uses page protectors, so you can insert half of your finished pages upside down. I used a 6" x 6" album—just perfect for one or two photographs and some journaling. (If you already scrapbook using 12" x 12" paper, all you have to do is cut each sheet into quarters to make it work in this size album.) JaNiese used "half-pint" sized pages (5.5" x 8.5") in a three-ring binder for her book (see Variation, p. 86).

2   Select a simple decorative element (such as a sticker, stamp or punch), as well as one or two colors of cardstock or patterned paper to use throughout your book.

3   Gather a few photos of each individual pictured separately and together.

Like Mother...

We both love to decorate our homes ... or at least improve our surroundings ... even a small guest bathroom must have a theme—this way it's easier to keep clean and is much more inviting. We think we both have a natural flair with decorating—although Mom is better.

We're so much alike!

Mom and I both love to exercise and the more I get around the more I see this as something quite unique. There are many who walk, run + bike, but we do it because it's good for them, really, honestly, truly like it. We would rather do a bike ride than "do lunch"

We Look Alike! . . . We are both beautiful and obviously humble about it ... It is a compliment when people say we're mother + daughter ... or they can tell   even sisters ☺

Like Daughter.

YOU CAN CREATE A WONDERFUL RELATIONSHIP book without the flip aspect, as my friend JaNiese Jensen did. JaNiese's husband Brent was inseparable from his twin brother Brian while growing up. Now, the twins live in different states, work in unrelated fields and have little in common when it comes to everyday life. JaNiese had several photographs from the boys' youth and wanted to preserve some of their shared memories and unique perspectives as twins in a small album.

Rather than have her book flip by placing each twin's responses in one half of the book, JaNiese put a question across the top of each page and mounted both twins' answers on the same page (who wants to separate twins?) She also included a photograph or two on each page from the boys' childhood. Since JaNiese planned to create two identical books and present one to each twin, she typed up the questions and answers on her computer, making the page assembly quick and easy. JaNiese also kept the page decorations very simple, using colored photo mats and, occasionally, decorative scissors, which also greatly speeded the creation of two identical albums.

One of my favorite things about JaNiese's album was a section she included with the brothers' memories of special people such as their grandparents. She had each twin list a few favorite childhood memories of each grandparent, which she then mounted together on a page with a photo of the grandparents.

JaNiese's "non-flip" relationship album is a great way to quickly compare two people's responses to the same question and enjoy some of their "together photos" at the same time. This format works especially well if you want to create a relationship book as a gift for two other people.

Have you decided yet who that extra-special person in your life is? Whether it's your mom, your sibling, or your best friend, creating a little flip book will capture more about your relationship than a few photos ever could!

"My Brother, My Twin, My Friend" by JaNiese Jensen

Album: 6" x 9" three-ring binder, Hiller

Scissors: Scallop edge, Provo Craft

Computer Fonts: CK Script, "The Best of Creative Lettering" CD Vol. 1, Creating Keepsakes; CK Journaling, "The Best of Creative Lettering" CD Vol. 2, Creating Keepsakes

I'm proud of you for..

Going against the odds and making a life in San Diego

Your success at work and with your family

Did I ever say Thank You for..

Being my friend, taking the time to call me on 5 cent Sunday, and caring about what I do.

Giving me a love for Broadway musicals.

My memories of

Grandma and Grandpa Kearl

I remember most a bowl of hard candy that Grandma Kearl always had and the parlor doors always closed. I also remember the back pantry off the kitchen that was always a little scary to go into.
Brian

I remember reading Go Dogs Go by Dr. Suess in the family room and Grandma sitting in her rocking chair. Eating sugar wafers, chocolate, strawberry and vanilla and not being allowed in the Parlor.
Brent

I admire you when..

You use reasoned, thoughtful thinking instead of jumping to conclusions.

I read your book of poems.

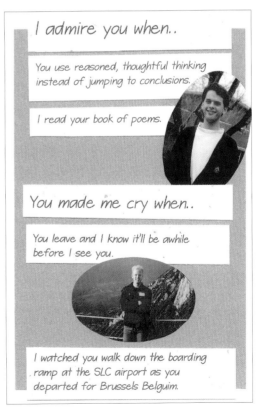

You made me cry when..

You leave and I know it'll be awhile before I see you.

I watched you walk down the boarding ramp at the SLC airport as you departed for Brussels Belguim.

Chapter 3

Scrapbooks for Children

THERE IS NOTHING HIGHER AND STRONGER AND MORE WHOLESOME AND USEFUL IN LIFE IN LATER YEARS THAN SOME GOOD MEMORY, ESPECIALLY A **MEMORY** CONNECTED WITH **CHILDHOOD**, WITH **HOME.**

—*FEODOR DOSTOYEVSKY*

Nine months is a long time to wait for anything in our fast-paced, drive-thru, instant gratification world. But this long anticipation of a baby is what makes its arrival so sweet and worth all the pain and discomfort of pregnancy. Children are truly a blessing.

This chapter contains six scrapbooking projects designed with children in mind. Start at the beginning, with family letters to a newborn babe or a celebration of a child's unique name. Take a few minutes to capture your family rituals, the songs you sing or the books you read together. If you feel overwhelmed by preserving a chronological record for your children, I'll show you how to accomplish this with just a few pages each year. All these things can become your children's "good memories connected with childhood and home."

I'VE GOT SOME PRETTY UNIQUE NAMES IN MY family line—from Addie and Antonetta to Wanda and Wilhelmina, with Elias, Electra, Honor, Narvella and Parley somewhere in the middle. I really wish I knew more about these names of my ancestors and why they were chosen. How much do you know about your name? How do you decide what to name your children? Some people have names chosen for years before their children are even born. Others research, debate and struggle up until the due date (or beyond!) to find just the perfect name. Either way, a name is an important gift we give our children that they carry with them the rest of their lives.

My husband and I have given each of our boys a great name. They have first and middle names that set them apart as individuals and a surname that reminds them that they are valuable members of something bigger—our family. I want each boy to know that he is just as unique and special as his name is, so I decided to create a small album for each one about his name. I plan to present it to them on a particular birthday, so they will look forward to receiving it. By creating "A Little Book about Your Name" like this, you can capture and celebrate who your children are, and they can learn a little about the special gift you gave them.

"Walter Clark Julian" by Stacy Julian

Blue Patterned Paper: Fabric Brights line, Keeping Memories Alive

Computer Font: CK Journaling, "The Best of Creative Lettering" CD Vol. 2, *Creating Keepsakes*

Pen: Zig Super Clean Color

Letter Stencil: ABC Tracers, Pebbles for EK Success

Other: Pictures of Superman and Clark Gable were printed from the internet; Clark Bar is an actual wrapper; "Clark" meaning page from Custom Creations by Names 'n Numbers (Salt Lake City, UT).

Great Grandpa & his Namesake

You are named after Walter Earl Clark, Dad's step grandfather. Walt married Doris Maas in 1943, after her first husband died of tuberculosis. Doris had a five year old daughter, Valerie (Dad's mom). Valerie was raised by Walt and she loved him so much, she took his name as her own.

When Dad was little, he and Grandpa Clark were the best of friends. When it came time to choose a name for you, Dad knew right away that he wanted to name you for this beloved man.

Walter Earl Clark

A LITTLE BOOK ABOUT YOUR NAME GUIDELINES

Begin your name book with a title page that has the child's full name, initials and a photo. The title page is also where you introduce the colors and design style you'll use throughout your book. I used a line of blue patterned paper for my son Clark's book. Something as simple as using the same pen and writing style throughout your book will also help give it some continuity.

At the front of the book, create the pages that are the most relevant to your child's given name. First, create a page (or a two-page spread) about why your child's name was chosen for him or her. Is the child named after someone in the family or someone famous? If so, be sure to include a photo of that person. Or is the name just simply one you really liked—and why do you like it so much? How did you first hear about the name?

Next, create a page or spread about the meaning of the child's name. There are many resources for finding out a name's meaning, including baby name books, web sites, and even stores and catalogs that specialize in

They have first and middle names that **set them apart** *as individuals and a surname that* reminds them *that they are valuable* **members** *of something bigger—* **our family.**

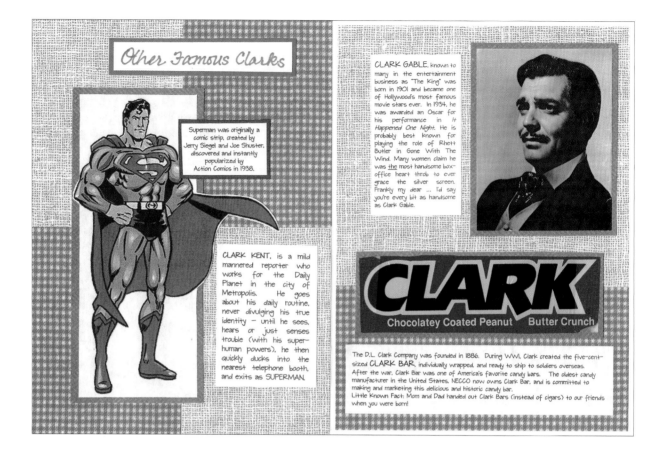

1 To make decorating this album really easy, use a monochromatic color scheme—various shades and patterns of a single color. Buy a dozen or so sheets in your selected color.

2 Gather several photos of your child, especially those that are "personality shots" capturing his or her individuality.

3 Select and purchase an album if needed. I used a 6.5" x 8.5" post-bound album for Clark's book. You might also consider having the album cover engraved with a title or the child's name. Several companies provide album engraving through the mail; a local trophy shop or bookstore might be able to provide a referral to places that can perform this service.

4 Decide which types of pages you want to include in your book and gather the needed information (see Guidelines, p. 91). I found the internet to be a great resource for historical tidbits.

5 Obtain a handwritten letter from Dad or Grandpa about the family surname.

name-related merchandise. Include the meaning of both the child's first and middle name. In Clark's book, I included a short definition from a baby book, as well as a longer, full-page version that I purchased at a craft fair (from a small company that provides computer print-outs). I also included a couple of fun photos that fit the descriptions of Clark as a warrior and a scholar.

There are several other name-related pages that you can create for your book. Choose one or all of the following page ideas:

• The Nickname Game—list all the nicknames that your child has been called and include a few fun photos.

• Friends that Share My Name—include photos of friends throughout the years that have the same name as your child. Leave some room to update it later as your child grows and meets new people.

• Other Famous Names—list famous people, places, and things that share your child's name, with photos (if possible) and a brief description. For example, in my son Clark's book, I featured Clark Kent, Clark Gable and the Clark candy bar.

• The "Write" Name for Me—have your child sign his name at different ages throughout his life. This page will be mostly blank at first, but you'll enjoy seeing how your child's handwriting changes through the years! Be sure to include his age next to each signature.

For the next part of your name book, create several "personality" pages. These are the pages that really showcase the unique personality of your child. Create a two-page spread for each letter of the child's first name—"Give me a 'C,'" "Give me an 'L,'" and so on. On each spread, list several adjectives starting with that letter that describe your child. For example, on the "A" page for Clark, I included descriptions such as affectionate, athletic, an animal lover, all boy, and adventurous. Then have fun filling in the page with photos to match the descriptions! Include photos of your child at various ages, and don't feel that you need to have a photo to go with every description you've listed. Keep the shape and matting of photos simple and clean (this is especially important when working with a small album).

Finally, conclude your album with a spread about the family surname. On one side, mount a picture of father and child together, or even a generational photo including a grandparent or great-grandparent. On the opposite side, you can include a handwritten letter from Dad or Grandpa about the family name. I've also included a poem titled "Your Name" by Edgar Guest which talks about the importance of a son honoring the name he received from his father. You might also want to include a brief history of the surname and a translation if it means something in another language.

What's in a name? A lot! Creating a book about your child's name is a wonderful way to give him a strong sense of self-worth and help him realize how important and unique he is. It's a gift your children will treasure—just like their name!

TYPICALLY, WHEN A FRIEND HAS A BABY—especially a first baby—people give the new parents a gift. But when my friend Heidi Nelson had her first baby, I did just the opposite. I called her up and asked her to do something for me! World's greatest friend, huh? Here she is with a new baby, short on sleep and energy, trying to make all the necessary adjustments to her life, and I call and give her an assignment (with a deadline, no less).

I asked Heidi to compile a "Dear Baby" album that I could share with you in this book. A "Dear Baby" album is a collection of letters addressed to a newborn baby from immediate and extended family members. I knew it wasn't a very nice thing to assign to a new mom—and a new scrapbooker to boot (Heidi's scrapbooking repertoire consisted of only six pages from her honeymoon)—and I knew that I would owe her big-time. But I also knew that this album would become very special to her and absolutely priceless to her daughter. When Heidi sent me her completed album, she included this letter to you, the reader:

> When I first began this project with a three-week-old baby, I thought that I was only trading sleep for scrapbooking time. But, the finished product is so precious to me now, as I look at my baby daughter, Ellie, and think about what this book may mean to her one day.
>
> The book shares our family values, time-honored truths, and generational wisdom with Ellie. The advice is written explicitly for her to read and learn from as she grows up. It provides a glimpse of her heritage, a window to the splendid extended family that she might not otherwise know.
>
> My heart is touched as I read each letter, knowing that a piece of the people I know and love will be around to embrace my daughter when she is older, just as they held her warmly as a babe in arms."

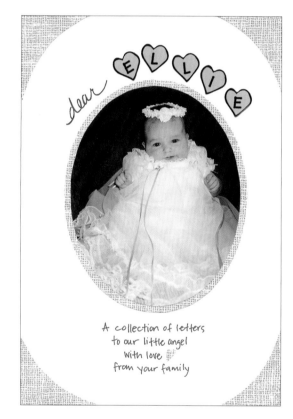

"Dear Ellie" by Heidi Nelson

Album: 6.5" x 8.5" post-bound, Dalee Book Co.

Patterned Paper: Title page and grandparent pages, Keeping Memories Alive; Parent pages, Unknown

Heart Stickers: Unknown

Pockets and Large Hearts (parent pages): Heidi's own designs

Other: Archival Mist from Preservation Technologies was used to de-acidify one of the letters.

The finished product
is so **precious**
to me now, as I look at
my baby daughter,
Ellie, and think about
what this **book** *may*
mean to her one day.

At the end of her letter Heidi thanked me (whew!) and added a post script to guard her book with my life!

If there's a new baby in your family (or even if the baby's not so new anymore), consider creating a "Dear Baby" album. The personal words and advice from extended family members will become a wonderful treasure as the baby grows up.

DEAR BABY ALBUM GUIDELINES

The title page for your "Dear Baby" album should include a photo of the baby, along with the baby's name. You might choose to use the "Dear Baby" title, substituting in the baby's name, as Heidi did for her title "Dear Ellie." Heidi also included a brief description and introduction to the album beneath her baby's picture.

The remaining pages in the album feature a photograph of a family member holding the baby and a pocket in which to tuck a handwritten note or letter from that person. Don't worry if you don't have a photo of every family member actually with the baby—simply include a recent photo of that person in any setting. (And feel free to update the page later on if you happen to get a photo of the two together—even if the baby's a little older.) Include the date the photo was taken somewhere on the page—and make sure the letter is dated as well.

Heidi placed the pages for herself and her husband (the parents) at the front of the album, and then orga-

nized her pages in two primary sections: paternal and maternal line (grandparents and great-grandparents) and extended family (aunts, uncles and cousins).

Try to use similar colors and page design throughout your album to provide some consistency. Heidi gave her album a very feminine, baby-girl feel by using pink paper and hearts throughout. However, she also managed to distinguish each individual spread by using a different pink patterned paper and a unique design aspect on each spread, such as placing a button on the letter pockets for the grandparents' pages. Heidi provided further consistency by quoting a sentence or summarizing a thought from each letter throughout the album—a great way to also add meaningful journaling to each page and serve as a reminder for what the letters contain.

Of course, the most important part of the album is the collection of letters from various family members (see the "Preparation" section). These letters might contain anything from favorite childhood memories to special advice and life-lessons learned. Encourage family members to use their own handwriting for their letters. If the letter won't fit in the pocket, you can store it inside the page protectors, between the back-to-back pages. *Tip:* Photo tape is a good adhesive choice for creating pockets strong enough to hold a note or letter.

Heidi received a few letters back on bright yellow notepad paper. She chose to store these letters inside the page protectors. Also, if you receive stationery or paper that isn't acid free, simply treat it with a deacidification spray. Remember—the content and handwriting of the letter is far more important than the size and color of paper used.

PREPARATION

1. Start gathering and taking pictures of your baby with the relatives you want to include in your book.

2. Contact your extended family members and ask them to send a letter for your "Dear Baby" album, along with a photo if you don't already have one. You may want to include some questions or prompts to help them when writing the letters. (If you want a specific type of information from them, make sure you ask for it.) Also, remind them to include the date, their full name and their relationship to your baby. If the letters will be part of the page's design, consider giving each family member a certain size or color of paper (acid free of course).

3. Select a color scheme for your album (baby colors are a good choice!) and purchase several sheets of coordinated or patterned paper.

4. Select and purchase an album. Heidi used a 6.5" x 8.5" post-bound album with a pink gingham fabric cover.

IF YOU DON'T WANT TO CREATE AN ENTIRE "Dear Baby" album, or if you don't have many extended family members to request letters from, you can still impart some of your own thoughts and wishes for your child. Even if your baby isn't a baby anymore, remember that it's never too late to write a letter to a child. So whether she's a toddler or a teenager, take a minute to write her a note, mount your handwritten words on a scrapbook page along with several photos of the two of you together and you've got a very meaningful layout!

Or, if you're compiling a baby book, you can include a "Dear Baby" page or section. This works well if you only have one or two letters from parents or grandparents. It's a wonderful way to capture some of the magical feelings and emotions that surround a new arrival.

Imagine baby Ellie as a young woman, reading through the letters written just for her as a baby. She might read this message from her great-grand-mother: *"My Mother (Martha Jane Miles Edwards) your great, great, grandmother often quoted to me: 'To thine own self be true and it must follow, as the night the day, thou canst not then be false to any man.' Always be grateful for your blessings and appreciate your heritage, which has brought so many good things to your life."* Even if Ellie has no memories of her great-grandmother, she will always have her words, counsel, and this treasured quote from Shakespeare to carry with her throughout her life. What a wonderful blessing!

"Dear Elizabeth" by Beth Walkulsky

Patterned Paper: Northern Spy

Computer Font: Collage Bold Italic, Print Artist

Calligraphy Pen: Marvy Uchida

Flower Embellishments: Classic Rose Decorative Paper Corners, Pebbles

Idea to Note: The title was created by enlarging and reversing the computer font, printing it out on the wrong side of a piece of pink paper, then cutting it out.

"Mommy & Ari" by Kristina Nicolai-White

Paper: Crafters Workshop

Border and Corner Stickers: Provo Craft

Leaf Rub-ons and Letter Stencil: Provo Craft

WHENEVER I LAY MY TWO-YEAR-OLD SON TREY down for a nap, he sticks one of his feet in the air. This isn't because he has tight hip flexor muscles, but rather because he's waiting for "kissy-foot." I'm not really sure how kissy-foot began, but it's a little ritual I share with Trey that requires me to—you guessed it—kiss his cute little sweaty foot before covering him up with his blanket. Sometimes I can get by kissing just one foot, and other times I'm stuck for ten minutes kissing both feet over and over. Either way it's kind of fun, a special moment in the middle of a usually hectic day when I can briefly connect to my boy and be repaid with the sound of his laughter.

I'll bet you also enjoy little family rituals in your home. Whether it's jumping in Mom and Dad's bed on Saturday morning or mixing up strawberry Kool-Aid every time you make popcorn, family rituals are less formal than our family traditions and seem to center around everyday routines. I've found that rituals often go unnoticed until one day a child asks, "How come we didn't . . . " or "Isn't it time for . . . ?" Some rituals are practiced every day, while others might be seasonal or associated with visiting a particular place. For example, whenever we stayed overnight at Grandma's house, she would warm our bath towels in the dryer so they would be toasty warm when we got out. (Even now, I always think of Grandma when I'm removing towels from the dryer.)

"The Julian Way" by Stacy Julian

Album: 5.5" x 8.5" half pint three-ring binder, Sew Be It

Black Sticker Letters: Pebbles in my Pocket

Punches: McGill (hand); Marvy Uchida (heart)

Patterned Papers: Mary Engelbreit (red check); All others, Close to My Heart

Small Apples: School stencil, Pebbles in My Pocket

Jumbo Circle Punch (egg centers): Family Treasures

School Stickers: Provo Craft

Rolling pin and eggs (circles on torn vellum): Stacy's own designs

Idea to Note: To make a photo hinge mat (like the one on page 101), cut a strip of cardstock 1" wide and the length of your photo. Fold it in half lengthwise. Slide the photo over the strip until its edge rests on the fold of the strip. Adhere the top of the folded strip to the top of your photo and then adhere the bottom side of the strip to your page (photo tape adhesive works well).

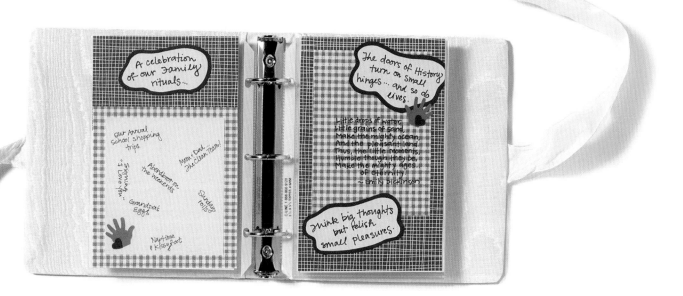

As corny as it might sound, rituals really do add a richness to our lives that should be remembered. It's just the "way" you do things, so why not capture it in a quick and easy little album? Your children will love to look through it over and over again as a fun celebration of their very own unique family.

FUN IDEA These little albums are perfect for taking along in the car, or keeping children occupied at places like the doctor's office or church. A grade school child could take one to share with his class when he's "star of the week." They are handy, fun, and very functional—I love scrapbooks that don't belong on a shelf!

FAMILY RITUALS ALBUM GUIDELINES

This project is especially suited for a smaller-sized album, since only one or two photos are used for each spread and it's a book you want your children to look at frequently. I used a 5.5" x 8.5" (half-size) album for my book. Create a title page for your album with a recent family portrait and a short title—I called mine "The Julian Way."

Rituals *really do* *add a* **richness** *to our lives that should be* **remembered.**

Grandma Hall makes the most delicious crescent rolls for Sunday dinner & special occasions. When Mom got married, she tried many times to get the Sunday rolls just right... but finally gave up and bought a bread machine. Now, Mom too makes really good rolls every Sunday.

Sunday Rolls

Sunday, March 26, 2000

Grandpa's eggs

Poached eggs for breakfast

Eat Your Eggs... they're Brain Food!

When mommy was growing up, grandpa and grandma would fix her eggs for breakfast whenever she wasn't feeling well or had to take a test at school.
Now, mommy fixes you eggs when she knows you need a little extra brain power to get you thru the day!
The best eggs are "for sure." grandpa's poached eggs – "eggstra" delicious!

A table of contents page or spread is optional for this little album. I created one for my book because I also wanted to include several quotes on celebrating life's little moments that really summed up the purpose of the album for me. For my table of contents, I simply left a large, blank journaling area to write in the title of each ritual page. This "random" table of contents format means I don't have to work in any kind of order—whenever I create a new ritual spread for my book, I simply write in the title!

Now, create a two-page spread for each family ritual that you want to highlight. On one side, include a photo or two that represents the ritual. Also, include a short title or name for your ritual. On the other side, add some journaling that explains what the ritual involves or gives a little history on how it got started.

FUN IDEA

If you don't have enough room for all the journaling you want to include, you can always hide some behind a

Our Annual **school** Shopping Trips

SCHOOL BUS

i ♥ school

Lift up the little bus to read all about it!

Spend a quiet moment making a list of a few rituals that you practice in your home. Start with just four or five—you can update your book over time as you think of more. Focus on those rituals associated more with your everyday routines rather than holidays or other special days.

If you don't have a photo that you can use to represent each ritual, start taking some! (I still have to capture our kissy-foot on film.)

Browse your local book or scrapbook store for a smaller album that catches your fancy (a spiral album would be fun!) Purchase a few decorative elements for enhancing each of your rituals and photos.

Locate a small family portrait to use on your title page (or make a reduced color copy of a larger one).

photo by creating a one-sided photo hinge mat, as I did for my school shopping trip page. (See Idea to Note on p. 98 for more information.)

For continuity in your album, try to use a similar design element on each spread. That doesn't mean you need to use the same color scheme throughout the book (I didn't). Instead, use one or two of the same design elements on each spread. For example, I created all of my titles using black sticker letters in a curved, "freehand" text box that I matted with a color matching another element somewhere else on the page. I also placed a strip of patterned paper horizontally across at least one of the pages in each spread.

Small things like rituals are an important part of each family. They're what makes your family unique and they'll give you and your children fond memories for years to come. Chronicling a few of your rituals in a small album is a great way to celebrate and enjoy them in the present as you also preserve them for the future.

School of Life Scrapbook

SEPTEMBER WILL ALWAYS MEAN "BACK TO school" for me. I have very vivid memories of this time of year: riding my bike to the elementary school every day to see if the classroom rosters had been posted yet, shopping for new shoes and clothes and gathering supplies like notebook paper and PeeChee folders. I still love the smell of new crayons and the feel of cooler fall days. It's so much fun now to share all the back-to-school excitement and emotions with my boys.

Another thing that I love about school is that it provides a perfect framework for capturing the chronology of a child's life. Chronological albums are an important part of recording your family's history, yet the task is often overwhelming—especially if you have several children and want to create a chronological album for each one. But when you can limit the scope of your job as family historian and follow a specific format, the task of compiling an all-inclusive chronological scrapbook becomes very realistic, even with three, four, or more children! That's where my "School of Life" albums come in.

THE "SCHOOL OF LIFE" CONCEPT

A "School of Life" album provides a brief chronological record of a child's life during his school years (from kindergarten to grade 12). Five scrapbook pages are created for each school year—two spreads and a pocket

"School of Life" by Stacy Julian

Album: 12" x 12" post-bound, Close to My Heart

TITLE PAGE *Patterned paper:* Close to My Heart

Lettering stencil: Close to My Heart

School rubber stamp: Close to My Heart

Pen: Zig Super Clean Color, EK Success

KINDERGARTEN SPREAD *Patterned paper:* Close to My Heart

Rubber stamps (apple, A+, letter K, books, pencil, flower): Close to My Heart

Pens: Zig Millennium 03 and 08, EK Success

FIRST GRADE SPREADS *Patterned paper:* Notebook and school designs, Frances Meyer; Green paper, Close to My Heart

Number Stickers: Déjà Views, The C-Thru Ruler Company

Pen: Zig Millennium, EK Success

Idea to Note: I used a Xyron laminating cartridge to laminate the class photos that are in the pockets. This helps protect them from fingerprints.

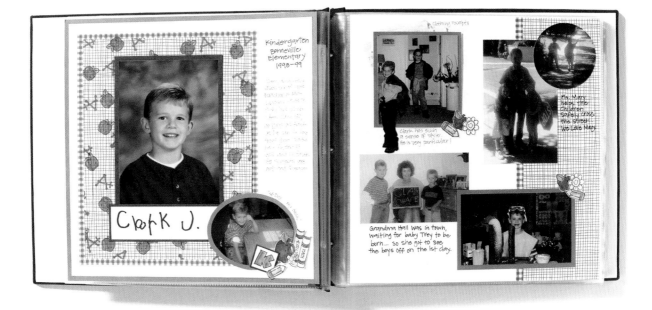

Kindergarten
Bonneville
Elementary
1998-99

Clark J.

Clark has such
a sense of style,
he is very particular!

Clothing roulpes

Ms. Mary
helps the
children
safely cross
the street!
We love Mary

Grandma Hall was in town,
waiting for baby Trey to be
born... so she got to see
the boys off on the 1st day.

School provides a
perfect **framework**
for capturing the
chronology *of a*
child's life.

page. The first spread captures aspects of *school*, while the second summarizes the events of everyday *life* that occurred during that year—hence my title "School of Life." The pocket page holds a few memorabilia items from that year, such as reports cards or artwork.

I think the trick to creating a chronological scrapbook is to edit your photographs and memories, follow a format and compile a summary of major events. If I tried to use every good photograph from every major event during every year of my children's lives, I could easily give them each more than twenty volumes when they leave home! While it would indeed be a treasure and a worthy pursuit, I'm not convinced it's the best use of all those photos or that the end result could be very easily transported—let alone enjoyed. Creating "School of Life" albums allows me to briefly chronicle each child's life. Then, when my children leave home, they will each be given three albums: their baby book and their two-volume "School of Life" set—one volume for the primary years and one for the secondary years. (By the way, boys, all the other books are mine—so don't even think of taking them until I'm at least 80. After all, I've got to have books to share with my grandchildren when they visit!)

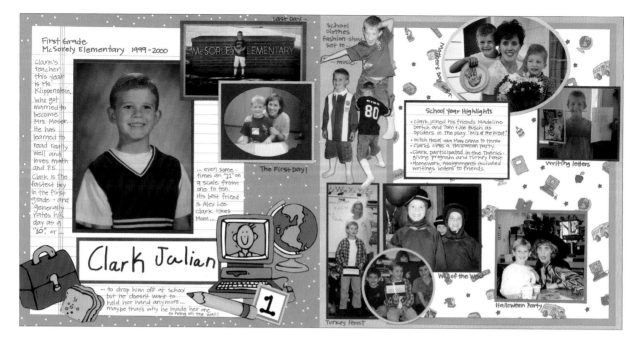

The "School of Life" concept has also given me the wonderful satisfaction of staying current with my children's lives. There is a strong desire among scrapbook enthusiasts to be "caught up" with their photos. With the "School of Life" format, all it takes is just five pages per year (per child) to be "caught up." This has allowed me to let go of what I call "scrapbooker's anxiety" and replace it with a sense of creative freedom to explore other meaningful projects and work in fun non-chronological ways.

The thought of keeping up a never-ending, chronological album with pages upon pages of photos scares me! I need to have a plan, be able to visualize the finished product and know exactly what's required of me. My "School of Life" books fit this bill for me—I hope you will also find something beneficial in them!

SCHOOL OF LIFE SCRAPBOOK GUIDELINES

I'm going to share with you one year from my son Clark's "School of Life" book. You'll see that it follows a pretty specific format. Please take the ideas that appeal to you and adapt them to your own needs. A larger-sized album works best for this book (mine is 12" x 12"), since it gives you lots of room for photographs and journaling.

Start by creating a title page with your child's name, an album title (such as "School

1 Select and purchase a large album for each child. I used a 12" x 12" post-bound album for each volume.

2 Throughout the school year, set aside any photos and school memorabilia that might be good candidates to include in the album.

3 Sometime during the school year, get your child to write his or her name on a piece of cardstock that you can later mount in the album. (If you forget, or if you're creating the album several years after your child started school, find a homework assignment or other project from that year and copy or trace your child's name—enlarging it if needed.)

4 Before the beginning of the next school year, sort through your photos and memorabilia and select those that match the criteria needed for each spread (see the guidelines section).

5 Choose one main color and one or two supporting colors from that year's school photo and purchase a few sheets of coordinating patterned paper, cardstock, and page embellishments.

of Life") and the years covered in that volume. I included a kindergarten photo of Clark and left room for his sixth-grade photo as a fun way to visually represent the time span recorded in that volume. I also labeled volume one as "The Primary Years."

Next, create the five pages for each year: a two-page "school" spread that captures aspects of school, a two-page "life" spread that summarizes events of everyday life during the year, and a pocket page to hold a few memorabilia items. I have certain things I want to include on each spread:

SCHOOL SPREAD

On the left side of the school spread, I include the following:

1. A 5" x 7" school photo.
2. The child's handwritten name.
3. A picture taken on the first day of school.
4. Journaling that includes the names of his teacher and best friend, his favorite subjects and a statement that reflects his general attitude toward school that year.

The right side of the school spread has a collage of five or six photographs that seem to represent that particular school year. I try to capture the style of school clothing and include photos of a school program or field trip, along with one or two other major activities or events. I might also include some journaling that lists the highlights of the year.

LIFE SPREAD

The life spread is made up of several photos (and descriptive journaling captions) from the following list:

1. A photo of my child's best friend.
2. One photo each from major holidays such as Halloween, Christmas and his birthday that year.
3. A photo depicting a talent or hobby, such as a team or individual sport photo.
4. One or two photos from major family events, such as new babies, weddings, reunions etc.
5. One or two family relationship shots—I love pictures that depict good times spent with siblings.
6. One or two personality shots that seem to really capture the child's interests, attitudes or achievements.

I use only one photo of each year's highlights and save the other photos to tell a more detailed story of special times in another album. (These more creative pages can be found in our Family Fun Library as described in the "Family Storybook" section of Chapter Two).

POCKET PAGE

The pocket page is the final page for each year. I select just a few items to place in the pocket, such as a report card, the class photograph, a spelling test or math worksheet, and a classroom newsletter or calendar. (I keep the rest of what comes home in a file box.) In addition to the pocket, this page also has room for mounting a few more photos or items of memorabilia. This is a great area for vacation or summer photos, a photo of your home, or some small item that reflects your child's interests that year, such as the little drawing that represents Clark's fascination with Pokémon.

I've placed the pocket page on the left side of the album and chosen to leave the right side blank except for a piece of patterned paper mounted on it. I have

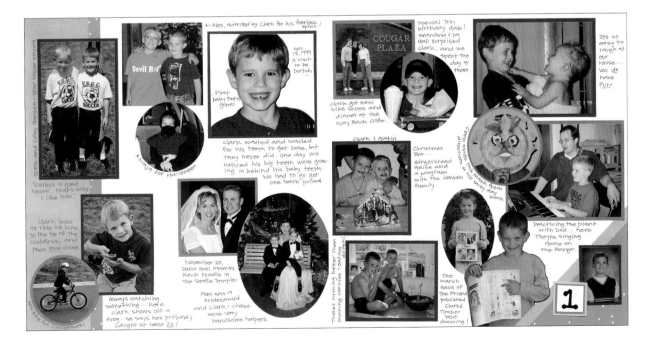

two reasons for doing this. First, because there is so much information on each page, the design can become very busy. A blank page helps to strengthen the division between each year (and give your eyes a rest at the same time). Second, my children may enjoy going back in later years and adding their own memories to each section. This additional page will give them the space they need to do that.

If you want to include additional material on this last page and create a spread with the pocket page, you could mount items such as an example of artwork created by your child that year (you may have to use a color copier to reduce a larger drawing or painting so it will fit).

FUN IDEA You can use birthdays instead of school years as the framework for your chronological album by creating a "Best Day of the Year" album. The first spread of each section would feature that year's birthday and would lend a theme and color scheme to the other pages for that section.

DESIGN TIPS

Because you're trying to condense an entire year into a few pages, it's important to pay attention to the design of your pages so they don't become too busy or cluttered. Here are a few design tips:

- Treat the 5" x 7" school photo as a focal point and pull color from it to use throughout all five pages for any patterned paper, photo mats, and so on.
- To add continuity within each section, mount a small square of cardstock containing the current grade number (or "K" for kindergarten) somewhere near the large school photo on the school spread. Then, repeat that square in the lower right corner of both the life spread and the pocket page, along with a wallet-size version of the 5" x 7" school photo. (This technique also makes it easy to know which year you're looking at as you browse through the completed album.)
- To help with the overall design and readability of each spread, pay special attention to both photo shapes and the colors used for mats and enhancements. Try to position similar colors or shapes in either opposite locations on your page or at the points of a triangle. For example, the first grade school spread uses a visual triangle of yellow photo mats (as well as oval-shaped photos). On the first grade life spread, green background paper is used on both the far left and far right sides of the spread. These similar elements help to balance and guide your eye through the layout.

IF YOU DON'T NECESSARILY WANT TO FOLLOW A SCHOOL format, but would like a concise version of your child's history, consider creating a "yearbook" album. My friend (and co-author) Gayle Humpherys created a yearbook album for her brother Tyler as a high school graduation gift. The album features a title page, followed by one spread for each year of Tyler's life. Gayle selected a handful of photos of Tyler from each year that represented major activities or events, as well as a few personality shots and a school photo. (You can have reprints or color copies made of your selected photos if needed.) She mounted the photos together with journaling excerpts taken from her family's newsletter that described Tyler's activities and accomplishments, along with humorous incidents.

FUN IDEA

Gayle also asked other family members to create their own scrapbook page as a "tribute" to Tyler on his graduation, and she included these pages in the second part of the album. These pages contained things like letters of appreciation, additional photographs, lists of admirable qualities, and fun memories. What a wonderful gift idea!

A yearbook album isn't necessarily a display of your scrapbooking creativity, but a simple summary of your child's life housed in one small album. (This album could easily be taken when the child leaves home.) A yearbook is a great project for a beginning scrapbooker, or for a seasoned veteran who wants to create a digest version of several already-completed volumes.

I love a "School of Life" approach for creating a simplified, chronological album. Now I can feel "caught up" with my children's albums and have more time to enjoy things with them like back-to-school shopping and crisp autumn days!

"Tyler's Graduation Yearbook" by Gayle Humpherys

Graduation Stickers: Mrs. Grossman's

Graduation Die Cut: Ellison

Scissors: Deckle edge, Family Treasures

Computer Fonts: CK Journaling, "The Best of Creative Lettering" CD Vol. 2, *Creating Keepsakes;* CK Anything Goes, "The Best of Creative Lettering" CD Vol. 1, *Creating Keepsakes*

Gold Pen: Zig Opaque Writer, EK Success

Colored Pencils: Memory pencils, EK Success

Favorite Songs Book

I HAVE FOND MEMORIES OF SINGING IN THE CAR with my family as we drove somewhere (especially to Grandma's house). Each of us would get a turn to choose a song and then Dad would start us out. It didn't matter if some of us were a little off-key or if the youngest ones didn't quite know all the words—it was great family-together time.

Several years ago, my sister Darci and I were up late one night reminiscing about our family car sing-a-longs and we started singing some of our old favorites. Then something terrible happened. I suggested we sing "MacNamara's Band"—it's such a great song and one of my dad's favorites—but we couldn't remember the words! We started over and over again, but nothing came. It was much too late to call Dad, so we went to bed hoping the words would come in the middle of the night.

In the morning, I asked my husband to name one of his family's favorite sing-a-long songs. "Jeremiah Was a Bullfrog," was his immediate response. When I asked him to sing it, he couldn't get past the second line. I vowed right then to get back in tune with the songs of my youth by compiling an album dedicated to our favorite songs. Now my family has a sing-a-long scrapbook that we actually keep in our car. In it you'll find the words to songs like the "I Love You" song from "Barney" (can you imagine forgetting those!), "You're a Grand 'Ole Flag" (we sing it whenever we see a big flag driving around town), and of course, "MacNamara's Band"—all three verses, complete with the "boom, booms."

"The Julian's Sing-a-Long in the Car Book" by Stacy Julian

Album: 8.5" x 11" three-ring binder, Frances Meyer

TITLE PAGE *Patterned Paper:* Frances Meyer

Computer Fonts: CK Chunky and CK Journaling, "The Best of Creative Lettering" CD Vol. 2, *Creating Keepsakes*

Car Stickers, Rub-Ons and Wave-edge Scissors: Provo Craft

BYU FIGHT SONG PAGE *Patterned Paper:* Colors by Design

Letter Stencil, Sticker Letters and Dress-up Stickers: Provo Craft

OLD MACDONALD PAGE *Scissors:* Mini pinking edge, Provo Craft

Letter Stencil, Sticker Letters and Dress-up Stickers: Provo Craft

Green Check and Handkerchief Paper: source unknown

Idea to Note: Stacy included hidden journaling behind the photo of the bagpipe player on the MacNamara's Band page.

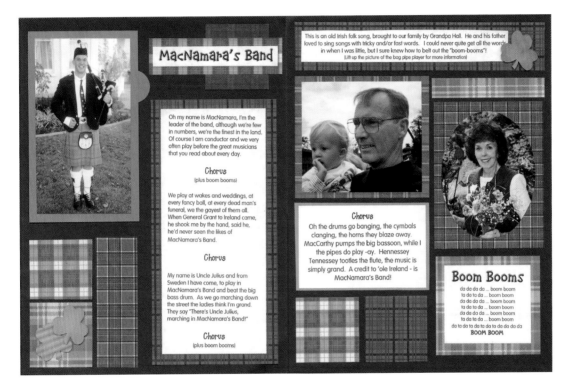

I have **fond**

memories *of singing*

in the car with my

family *as we* **drove**

somewhere (especially to

Grandma's *house).*

If you have songs that you loved to sing as a child or still sing with your children now, write them down in a favorite songs scrapbook. Recording them in an album not only ensures you'll always have the lyrics handy, it also allows you to preserve some of your memories associated with those songs. Plus, your children will love to look at the personalized pages as they sing along!

FAVORITE SONGS BOOK GUIDELINES

To start off your songbook, create a title page and a table of contents. Since I intended my book to be kept in the car, I designed these introductory pages around a car "sing-a-long" theme. You might title your album something as simple as "Favorite Family Songs" and use more music-oriented decorations. I used patterned paper that coordinated with my album cover (polka dots and stripes), and chose bright, fun colors that work well for a children's album. Since each of your song pages will likely use different colors and themes, coordinating these initial pages pulls the whole project together and gives it a sense of completion.

In the table of contents, you can divide your list of favorite songs into categories or sections. I used two divisions: "Our Favorites" and "Holiday Songs." As you make your song list, be sure to ask your family—and especially your children—to contribute one or two song suggestions. Consider songs from these categories:

- Pre-school and childhood favorites
- Traveling songs from your youth
- Traditional cultural songs
- Patriotic selections—why not teach your kids the national anthem!
- Christmas carols or other holiday songs
- A favorite hymn or two
- School fight songs
- Any original songs written by a member of your family.

FUN IDEA I made up a silly song for each of my children when they were babies, so I included a personality spread in our book dedicated to each child with the words of their song!

After you've decided what songs to include, list them in your table of contents. It doesn't really matter what order you put them in or how you categorize them. Don't worry if you can't complete all the song pages right away. I still have several songs in my table of contents that I haven't created pages for yet. As you finish the pages in the future, just place them in the book according to their order in the table of contents.

FUN IDEA I also added a few song-related quotes to my table of contents as little reminders of the fun and value of singing.

Now, create a two-page spread for each song—choose maybe five songs to begin with. For each song, begin with the song title and lyrics. Then add a couple of photographs, some documentation and a few fun enhancements. Some of the things you might include are a list of the places you often traveled as a child, a picture of your family car, or a photo of the person you think of most when you sing that particular song. If the song has ever been recorded professionally, you could add the name of the artist or group that made it popular. Historical tidbits are always interesting to include. You might also write down some of the random memories that come to mind as you sing a familiar tune.

Use the theme of each song to determine the design and feel of the spread. Have fun designing these pages! I tried to use bright, fun colors to give our book a happy, inviting feel for children.

FUN IDEA You can add a memory button to one or more of your song pages with a portion of the melody, a grandparent singing a verse or even your toddler singing a familiar chorus. Or, create a cassette tape recording of your kids singing the songs in your book. Then, if no one else is singing, one child could still keep himself busy for several miles with your homemade sing-a-long tape and book!

Compiling a favorite songs album is a fun way to remember old songs, teach your children new ones, and simply enjoy singing time together. The next time I get the urge to sing "MacNamara's Band," I won't have to worry about waking up my dad for the words—I'll know right where to look. (And my kids already have the "boom, booms" down pat!)

Lovingly made and presented
to my children
for Christmas 1997
~Stacy Julian

PREPARATION

1 Make a list of five or ten of your family's favorite songs. (See Guidelines, p. 109, for more direction.) You can always add more songs to your songbook later.

2 Write down the song lyrics—and don't forget the "doo-dahs" and "da da da dums!" If you can't remember all the words, the internet is a great resource.

3 Select and purchase an album and a few sheets of coordinated paper and enhancements. I used an 8.5" x 11" album.

4 Include a dedication to your favorite singers (see detail of my dedication page, left).

Chase and Clark at Wheeler Farm '97

OLD MacDonald had a Farm

OLD MacDonald had a farm.

EIEIO

and on this farm, he had some _____ Fill in the blank.

EIEIO

oink   neigh   moo

with a ___ ___ here, and a ___ ___ there, here a ___, there a ___, everywhere a ___ ___.

OLD MacDonald had a farm

EIEIO

More animals to try:
Ducks   Cats
Chicken   Dogs
Sheep   Mice

Favorite Books Album

I'M READING *HARRY POTTER* TO MY BOYS THIS summer. We all love it! We snuggle up on the bed and enter the wacky world of wizards and wands. We wonder what it would be like to ride high on a broom and then suddenly dive out of the sky in a wild game of quidditch. I'm sure my boys will be able to recall images of Harry Potter's adventures for many years to come, much like I remember the stories of Pippie Longstocking, Laura Ingalls Wilder, and Nancy Drew. It's nice to know that even in our world of satellite TV and Nintendo, a book can still grab the attention of a little boy and occupy his mind and imagination long after its cover is closed.

Books have a way of staying in our memories, but how often do we share those memories with others? At the age of eight, my mother-in-law received a copy of the book *Smoky* from her grandparents. I inherited this book several years ago when she passed away. Since my boys never got to know their grandmother personally, reading this book to them is like sharing a part of her. I only wish we knew what she enjoyed most about it and how it affected her.

If you enjoy sharing books in your family, why not start your very own family book club, as I did? When I found a beautiful tapestry binder with a book pattern, I knew it would a perfect place to document the books we read in our family, record where we got them, highlight what we liked about each one and relate any other memories or stories associated with them. While my intent was to create this album for my children, it's not solely for children's books. You can record any type of books your family reads and enjoys in your favorite books album.

"Family Book Club" by Stacy Julian

Album: 8.5" x 11" Living Oak tapestry binder, Hiller Industries

Patterned Paper: Lasting Impressions

Book Die Cut: Ellison

Letter Stencil: Provo Craft

Flower Stickers (Fairytale page): Me & My Big Ideas

Decorative Edge: Family Treasures

Ideas to Note: Ribbon was used to create bookmarks in the book die cuts and jute was used to tie a quote written on vellum paper on the subtitle pages.

__Books__ have a way of staying in our memories, *but how often do we* share those *memories with others?*

FAVORITE BOOKS ALBUM GUIDELINES

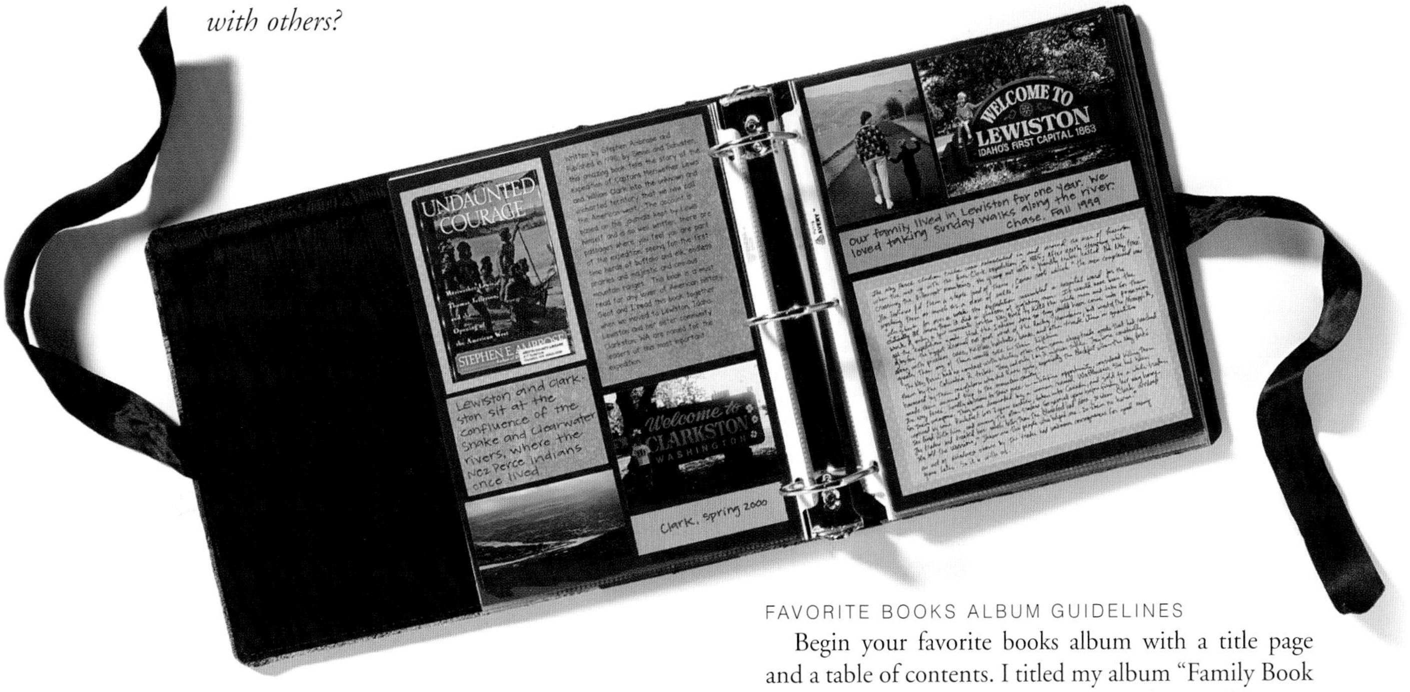

Begin your favorite books album with a title page and a table of contents. I titled my album "Family Book Club," since I wanted it to be a compilation of favorite book recommendations from every member of our family. (For example, when my husband finishes a book, I ask him if it's one to include in our book club. If so, I have him write up a paragraph about the book, revealing one or two things he enjoyed about it.)

The table of contents is actually a two-page spread. On the left side, create a decorative page listing the book categories you want to use in your album. I selected four main categories: Fiction, Non-fiction, Children's Literature, and Holiday Favorites. On the right side, place an alphabetical list of the book titles featured in your album. After each title, include a capital letter denoting which category it's in, such as "C" for Children's Literature. Since this list is frequently updated, I simply typed it up on the computer so I can add new books and print out a new list whenever I need to. I inserted the printed page in a page protector by itself (without any type of decoration) as the right side of the table of contents spread.

Then, create a subtitle page for each of the book categories you've chosen. I used a different color for each subtitle page (heading, mats and other page decorations) to match the color on the table of contents. I also included a favorite quote related to books or reading.

Now, you're ready to create the pages for each book on your list. Depending on the length of the book and the amount of information you want to include, you can create anywhere from a single paragraph to a multipage spread about each book. For example, I made a spread of some of my boys' favorite bedtime stories and featured three books per page (six books total), with only a paragraph and small picture of the book cover for each one. For other books, I've created an entire two-page spread. Remember—don't feel like you have to create pages for all the books on your list right at first. Start with a few book pages and continue updating your album as your time and energy allow.

Think about each book you're highlighting and jot down some notes about why it's one of your favorites. Use these questions to help:

1. Where did you get this book? Was it a gift? If so, who gave it to you?

2. Did someone significant recommend it? Why?

3. What was happening in your life at the time you first read it? How old were you? What kind of impression did the book have on you at that time? What is your memory of reading it now?

4. Why has this book continued to be a favorite throughout your life?

5. How have you shared this book with others? How has it affected them, or your relationship with them?

6. What would you tell your children and grandchildren about this book? What have you learned by reading it? Why do you want them to read it?

Then, in addition to some of the information above, consider including one or two of the following on your book page:

• A reduced color copy or scan of the book's cover or some of the illustrations

• A photo of yourself at the age you read this book, people who read it to you, or you reading to your children

• A favorite bookmark

• A photo of a person, place or activity that's related to the book's storyline

• A brief biography of the author or a historical sketch of the book

• Trivia about the book, such as when it was published and how many copies have been sold

• A quote or selected text from the book

• The movie title and your reaction to any screen versions of the book that have been made.

To provide continuity throughout your album, try to

use a simple color scheme and related design elements. For example, I used colors from my binder's tapestry throughout the album and used black cardstock for all my pages. I color-coded the four book categories on the table of contents and then used the appropriate color on the subtitle page, as well as somewhere on each book page in that category (for mats or other design ele-ments). I also repeated the book die cut from the title page on each category subtitle page.

ADDITIONAL PAGE IDEAS

In addition to creating pages about books you've read consider these "extra" pages for your book album:

- If you acquired your love of reading from a family member (such as a parent or grandparent), create a page featuring a photo of them, a list of their three all-time favorite books and some of your "reading" memories of them.
- Use your album to keep track of books you've lent out. Add a page where you can record the book's title, the borrower's name and phone number, along with a place where they can share their opinion of the book when they return it.
- If you regularly receive books as gifts, let your album function as a place to record the title of each book and the giver's name. When an object (like a book) is connected to a friend or loved one it takes on much greater meaning. Don't let this meaning get lost over time.

FUN IDEA Make an extended family book club album at your next family reunion. Simply tell each family member that their "ticket" to dinner is a scrapbook page about their favorite book! Place the pages in a big binder according to generation and see who stands in line for a copy!

Scrapbooks for the Holidays

There's nothing like a holiday for bringing together friends and family in the spirit of celebration. Daily routine gladly gives way to a magical atmosphere of anticipation and remembering. Preparations are plenty and decorations abound. Memories are hidden in each sight, sound, and smell. No matter what the occasion or time of year, the traditions and celebrations connect us a little more to the past, help us cherish and enjoy our present relationships, and renew our anticipation of future festivities.

The simple scrapbooks in this last chapter are about the meaningful aspects of holiday celebrations. Read on, and see how to capture the recollections of past and present generations from all the holidays you enjoy celebrating. I'll show you a great way to record your important traditions and create a handy holiday planner at the same time! You can involve your family and friends as you each express thanks annually in a gratitude journal. Learn some quick, easy ideas for storing and displaying Christmas greetings from friends. And why not start a scrapbook as a way to exchange annual updates among extended family members?

All the Holidays Scrapbook

DO YOU KNOW WHAT DECEMBER 25TH, OCTOBER 31st, February 14th, and August 26th have in common? They're all holidays! That's right. August 26th—National Cherry Popsicle Day, of course! If you're not familiar with August 26th, chances are you don't know about March 26th either: Make Up Your Own Holiday Day—and I'm not making that up. Why not try observing National Relaxation Day on August 15th, or join with me in requiring children everywhere to celebrate May 10th, Clean Up Your Room Day?

If there's one thing we love to do, it's to celebrate holidays, large and small. And whether it's a religious observance, a historical event, or even a national hero's birthday, we seem more inclined to pull out our cameras on these special days. Even if the scrapbook bug hasn't bitten you yet, you probably have plenty of holiday photographs stashed away somewhere. Why not compile the best of them in a fun album that celebrates all of your family's favorite holiday memories?

Putting together an "All The Holidays" scrapbook is easier than you might think. To demonstrate this, I gave my friend Jodi Olson just one weekend to begin compiling her family's album, with a few guidelines. First, I wanted her to use design elements that could be applied to a title page, subtitle pages for each holiday, and simple "fill-in" section pages that would be added over time. Second, I asked her to emphasize multi-generational memories more than chronology—no need to

"The Olson Family Holiday Scrapbook" by Jodi Olson

Album: 8.5" x 11" Sew Be It, Timeless Tapestry

Patterned Paper: Keeping Memories Alive

Letter Stencil: Block Tracer, Pebbles in My Pocket

Computer Fonts: LD Delightful, Inspire Graphics; CK Cursive, "The Best of Creative Lettering" CD Vol. 2, *Creating Keepsakes*; Doodle Basic, Cock-a-Doodle Design

Sticker Letters ("Trick or Treat"): White Dot Alphabitties, Provo Craft

Punches: Large balloon (eggs), circle (balloon), and birch leaf (turkey wing), Family Treasures; Teardrop (watermelon seeds and candles) and hole punch (berries), McGill; Holly punch, Forever Memories; Circle & small star (bat), small apple (trick or treat bag), Marvy Uchida

Scissors: Grass edge, Provo Craft

Templates: Watermelon, gingerbread man and cake, Pebbles in My Pocket; Pumpkin, Oval Coluzzle: Turkey, based on Provo Craft; Stocking, based on Pebbles in My Pocket

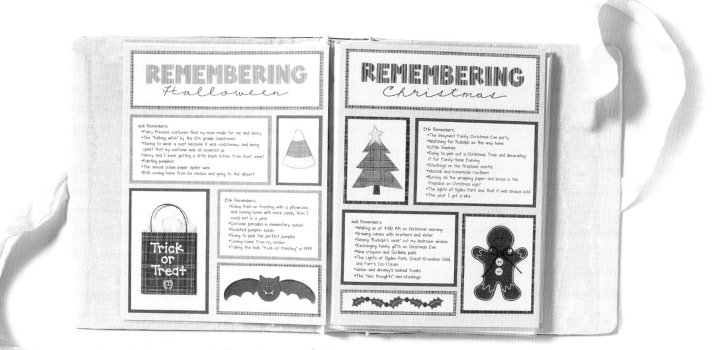

arrange photos by date or year. And most importantly, I told her to focus on capturing the meaning of each holiday in her home rather than worrying so much about completing pages. I knew Jodi would do a great job, but the outcome far exceeded my expectations!

This is the perfect project if you're a beginning scrapbooker for three great reasons: it only requires using a handful of your best holiday photos; you don't have to worry about putting photos in chronological order; and the simple format makes it a snap to keep your album updated!

ALL THE HOLIDAYS SCRAPBOOK GUIDELINES

To begin your "All the Holidays" scrapbook, create a title page that includes an album title and small decorations to represent the various holidays featured in your scrapbook (such as rubber stamps, stickers or die cuts). The design, colors and format of your title page set the mood and style for the rest of your book. Jodi's quilt-like title page gives her entire album a homespun and charming feel. She represented each holiday with a small paper-pieced design (created with patterned

If there's one thing we **love** *to do, it's to* celebrate **holidays,** *large and small.*

paper), which she arranged in a quilt-type pattern, along with the title and a great quote that captures the album's purpose. Jodi chose a natural beige paper as a background color throughout her album—this color is a perfect neutral to support and coordinate with the wide range of holiday colors.

Next, create a subtitle page for each of the individual holidays you want to feature in your album. You can include whatever holidays your family observes. Jodi created album sections for Christmas, Valentine's Day, Easter, the Fourth of July, Halloween, Thanksgiving and Family Birthdays. On each subtitle page, list the holiday name and add two or three decorations that coordinate with the main title page. Notice how Jodi used the same paper-piecing technique to create a few holiday-related decorations that are different from those on the title page.

The subtitle page is also a great place to add some journaling and really make the page meaningful. Jodi titled her pages "Remembering ..." (inserting the appropriate holiday name) and then listed a few of her childhood memories of that holiday, as well as some from her husband Erik. These simple lists really make you want to turn the page and find out more! You could also include some of your family's traditions for that holiday or get every family member to list some of their favorite things associated with the holiday—everything from the sites and smells to

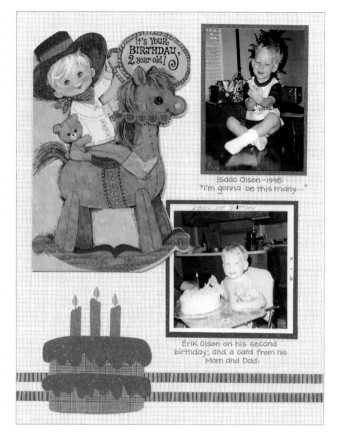

Isaac Olson—1998
"I'm gonna be this many..."

Erik Olson on his second birthday; and a card from his Mom and Dad.

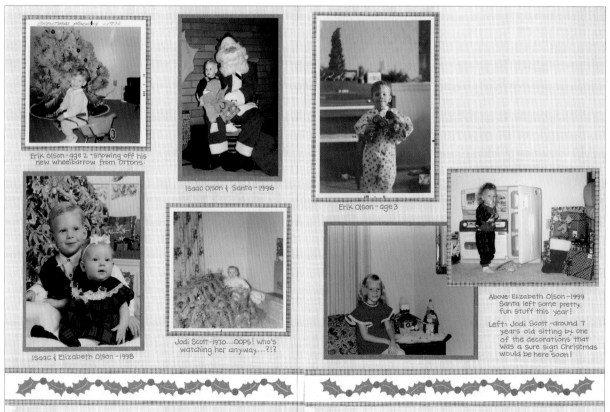

Erik Olson—age 2—showing off his new wheelbarrow from Ortons.

Isaac Olson & Santa—1996

Erik Olson—age 3

Isaac & Elizabeth Olson—1998

Jodi Scott—1970...OOPS! who's watching her anyway...?!?

Above: Elizabeth Olson—1999 Santa left some pretty fun stuff this year!

Left: Jodi Scott—around 7 years old sitting by one of the decorations that was a sure sign Christmas would be here soon!

August 26th

Chase observes...

National Cherry Popsicle Day.

activities and people you get to visit with.

Now, you're ready to create the "fill-in" pages for each holiday. All you need to do is add a simple border design to a blank page and you're ready to mount your photographs! These fill-in pages can be created ahead of time (as blank pages with just the border design), or you can create them as you need them. Choose a simple border that coordinates with the holiday's subtitle page design and make sure you leave plenty of room on each page for photographs and journaling. Jodi created her border by repeating one of the designs from the subtitle page along the bottom of the page. Use the same border on each fill-in page for that holiday, and you'll never have to design new pages for your album again!

Once your border is in place, you can mount your photos and add a little journaling. Use only one or two photos from each year and don't worry about filling up each page completely—the idea is to simply add a few photos every so often. I asked Jodi to purposely leave a blank on her Christmas fill-in page to illustrate how easy to update it with additional photographs. Keep the photo shapes simple and mount them on cardstock or patterned paper if you want. Include photos from your own childhood as well as more recent photos. Notice how Jodi purposely placed photographs of herself and her husband as children alongside current photos of their own children. You might also want to include one or two memorabilia items as well, such as a favorite card, or recipe. Don't forget to label each photo.

FUN IDEA A blank holiday album makes a great gift. Simply create the title page, subtitle pages (with blank journaling areas for memories) and a few fill-in pages for each holiday with the border in place. All the recipient needs to do is add her own memories and photographs!

So dig out those holidays photos one weekend and get to work preserving your memories in a holiday scrapbook. It's sure to become a featured decoration in your home all year round, a reminder of happy celebrations and the best of times!

PREPARATION

1 Make a list of the holidays you want to feature in your album. Include the holidays and other occasions (like birthdays) that your family enjoys celebrating.

2 Begin gathering photos and memorabilia for each holiday section. Include photos from your youth as well as more recent photos. Spend some time carefully editing and selecting photographs that best represent your holiday memories over time.

3 Select and purchase an album, if needed. (Jodi used an 8.5" x 11" album.) Also purchase coordinating holiday embellishments. Jodi used the same line of patterned paper and the same paper-piecing technique throughout her album to unify the overall design.

EVERY SPRING BEFORE EASTER, WE PLAN A DAY to clean up our yard. My boys willingly pitch in because when we're done we can go inside and schedule our annual Easter egg hunt! I've enjoyed the tradition of Easter egg hunts since I was a girl. My family had two acres of forest behind our house, which made for a real hunt. Mom would tie a ribbon between two trees near the entrance to the "woods" and as soon as the ribbon was cut, half the neighborhood would scatter searching for candy. My dad did such a thorough job hiding candy, it wasn't unusual to find little foil eggs up through Labor Day!

I love traditions and I live for holidays. So it's not surprising that holiday traditions are a big deal at our house. We honor traditions from my youth, like making our own Halloween costumes. We borrow traditions from friends, like getting Leprechaun kisses on St. Patrick's Eve, and we make up brand new traditions, like having a special Valentine's Day breakfast and getting something red to wear. The only problem with all this holiday fun is that it takes quite a bit of organization—and if there's one thing I don't like, it's forgetting to carry out some small detail of holiday observance. My solution? A functional holiday traditions scrapbook!

This album has become one of my favorites. It has one section for each major holiday, is very easy to assemble and requires no updating once it's complete. I keep it in the kitchen, where my boys and I can use it to anticipate and plan for the next holiday. In addition to fun photographs and memories, it contains a laminated checklist that I can pull out and put on my fridge with menu items to prepare, decorations to put out and other to-do's. There's even a place for me to file away new ideas that I've

"Holiday Traditions" by Stacy Julian

Album: 8.5" x 11" binder with front plastic pocket, Wilson Jones

Divided Sheet Protectors: Stampin' Up!

Sticker Letters: Provo Craft

Photo Frames: Frame-Ups and Frame-Ups Corners, My Mind's Eye

Die Cuts: Frame-Ups Die Cuts, My Mind's Eye

Dolls: Frame-Ups Friends, My Mind's Eye

Patterned Paper: Fabric Brites, Keeping Memories Alive

Punches: Family Treasures

Computer Font: VAG Rounded Thin, Corel WordPerfect

Other: Xyron machine, for laminating the holiday checklist pages

Any collection of holiday
memories *and*
traditions *will become a*
family treasure.

collected and clipped from magazines, like party games, kid's crafts and recipes. This scrapbook is my special holiday "planner" that helps me create an atmosphere in our home where fun and lasting memories can be made.

HOLIDAY TRADITIONS GUIDELINES

Any collection of holiday memories and traditions will become a family treasure, so I hope you'll borrow some of my ideas, add some of your own and present the whole thing with your own signature style. My boys love to sit up at the kitchen counter and look through our book as they talk about the next holiday. Please don't be too overprotective of this book. It will probably get flour spilled on it and be covered with little fingerprints, but remember, this is a functional book meant to be used and enjoyed. The important thing is to start today!

One of my goals with this project was to achieve a clean, simple look that required very little creative energy and followed a consistent format. To make the album assembly quick and easy, I used sticker letters, divided sheet protectors and pre-made die cuts, photo frames and dolls.

First, create a title page that establishes the overall design and style you'll use in your book. It's fun to use

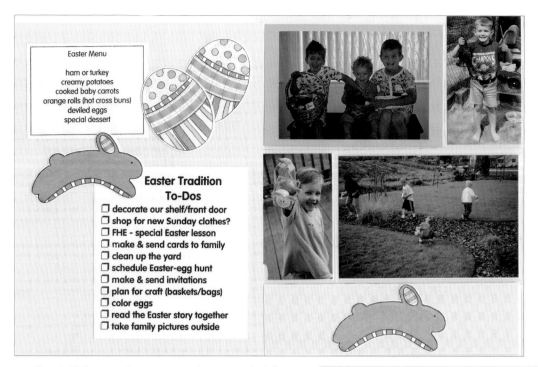

Easter Menu

ham or turkey
creamy potatoes
cooked baby carrots
orange rolls (hot cross buns)
deviled eggs
special dessert

**Easter Tradition
To-Dos**

- decorate our shelf/front door
- shop for new Sunday clothes?
- FHE - special Easter lesson
- make & send cards to family
- clean up the yard
- schedule Easter-egg hunt
- make & send invitations
- plan for craft (baskets/bags)
- color eggs
- read the Easter story together
- take family pictures outside

small embellishments that represent the various holidays featured in your album. I titled my album "Holiday Traditions" and decorated it with several ready-made holiday "kids" to give my book a bright, fun and colorful feel.

Next, create a subtitle page for each holiday you want to include in your book. Select one photograph that captures some aspect of that particular holiday

PREPARATION

1 Select the holidays you want to feature in your album. Include unique holidays and occasions that have traditions surrounding them. You don't have to include every major holiday. I chose the following ones: Christmas, Valentine's Day, St. Patrick's Day, Easter, May Day, Mother's and Father's Day (combined), Fourth of July, Halloween, Thanksgiving, and Birthdays.

2 Select and purchase a three-ring binder, several divided sheet protectors and any patterned paper and embellishments to coordinate with each holiday.

3 Make a list of the traditions your family observes with each holiday, then sort through your photos and select several that represent these traditions. (Start taking some photos if you haven't captured a tradition on film yet.) If it's too overwhelming to do all the holidays at once, see Guidelines, p. 123, for tips on working on one holiday at a time.

Every year the Easter Bunny hides our baskets and when we wake up, we have to search for them!

Our Annual Easter-egg Hunt!

Easter celebrates the resurrection of Jesus Christ.
We believe that because Jesus was resurrected, we will also live again. In the 24ᵗʰ chapter of Luke in the New Testament, we read about Jesus' disciples coming to the tomb early Sunday morning and finding it empty. Confused, they were greeted by two angels who asked them ...
"Why seek ye the living among the dead? He is not here, but is risen.."

**Easter Decorations
Making Cookies
Easter F.H.E.
Coloring Eggs
Going to Church
Watching Easter Videos**

There is always one special plastic egg in our baskets. Unlike the other candy filled ones, this egg is empty. When we open it, we remember with love and gratitude the empty tomb!

Lighting our Easter Train!

and mount it on the page with the holiday name and a few enhancements. By following the same format for each subtitle page—changing only the photograph, colors and individual enhancements to match the holiday—these pages come together very quickly and provide continuity to your album. For example, on each of my subtitle pages I used a pre-made photo frame, a strip of patterned paper behind the holiday title (created with sticker letters), two or three die cuts (pre-cut and colored), and a few small coordinating punched shapes (like eggs, stars or leaves). I pulled two or three colors from the enhancements to use throughout that holiday section.

The rest of each holiday's section contains the following pages:

CHECKLIST PAGE. This page contains your holiday "to-do" checklist. List all the things you need to do to prepare for that holiday, from menu items to decorations to special places to visit. I typed my list on the computer, then mounted it on a piece of patterned paper with a few coordinating enhancements. Laminate your checklist so you can place it on the refrigerator each year. I store my checklist page back-to-back with the holiday subtitle page.

FILL-IN PAGES. These pages contain photographs and journaling to highlight traditions associated with each holiday. To save me from having to design a creative layout for each page, I used divided sheet protectors with

five or six pockets. In the pockets, I insert photos (sometimes matted), journaling blocks (sometimes mounted with an embellishment or small photo), or occasionally a die cut simply mounted by itself on a piece of cardstock. I also try to use these pages to record the religious and cultural significance of our holiday traditions. This is something I find hard to do with other holiday scrapbook pages, yet it's very easy and appropriate in this book. Don't leave out the reasons behind your traditions—they are the most important aspect!

I generally use just two fill-in pages for each holiday (each divided protector holds quite a few memories). If you decide to update your scrapbook in the future, you could simply exchange some of the individual photos or journaling blocks (very easy), or add another divided sheet protector.

NOTES AND IDEAS PAGE. The last page of each section is a place for you to file any notes or ideas for future holiday celebrations. It's a simple sheet protector containing a white piece of cardstock. I decorated the cardstock by repeating the strip of patterned paper from the subtitle page across the top and using one of the die cut "kids" along with the small title "Notes & Ideas." I cannot tell you how happy this one page makes me! I now have somewhere to put magazine articles, ideas from the internet, and even tickets to holiday events. If I find a

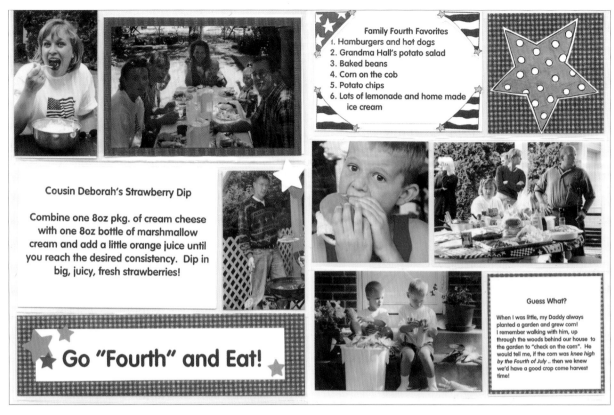

Family Fourth Favorites
1. Hamburgers and hot dogs
2. Grandma Hall's potato salad
3. Baked beans
4. Corn on the cob
5. Potato chips
6. Lots of lemonade and home made ice cream

Cousin Deborah's Strawberry Dip

Combine one 8oz pkg. of cream cheese with one 8oz bottle of marshmallow cream and add a little orange juice until you reach the desired consistency. Dip in big, juicy, fresh strawberries!

Guess What?

When I was little, my Daddy always planted a garden and grew corn! I remember walking with him, up through the woods behind our house to the garden to "check on the corn". He would tell me, if the corn was *knee high by the Fourth of July* .. then we knew we'd have a good crop come harvest time!

★ **Go "Fourth" and Eat!** ★

fun idea I want to try, I jot it down or make a copy, grab my handy Holiday Traditions book and file it away!

If you don't want to finish your holiday traditions book all at once, work one holiday section at a time. As the holiday approaches, make all your to-do lists and plans as usual, making notes as the season progresses. Which recipes do you prepare? What decorations do you display? Are there particular places you visit? As you participate in your annual observances, keep a little notebook with you and jot down the meaning of specific traditions. Pay special attention to capturing each tradition on film and write out the reasons you do the things you do. After the holiday is over, finish compiling that holiday's section by inserting photographs and journaling into the divided page protectors. Next year when that holiday rolls around, you'll be fully prepared and ready to carry out all your plans!

Planning for and carrying out holiday traditions is one of the most important things we can do for our families. Traditions are often very simple activities that strengthen the ties between generations and give us the opportunity to teach our children about values and beliefs. Whatever your special traditions are, make an effort to celebrate and record them in a scrapbook! (And let your scrapbook be a planning "helper" to make sure you don't miss any of the important details.)

IN 1863, ABRAHAM LINCOLN ISSUED A PROCLA-mation establishing the last Thursday of November as a national day of Thanksgiving. In 1991, I issued my own proclamation establishing Thanksgiving as the Julian's day for remembering our blessings in writing. Thus started our family's "Thanksgiving Gratitude" book. This is a wonderful project to make your Thanksgiving celebration more meaningful and far reaching. It's a scrapbook version of a gratitude journal, a concept introduced by Sarah Ban Breathnach in *Simple Abundance* and popularized on a large scale by Oprah Winfrey. I promise that this is a very easy album to begin and keep updated. In a matter of a few short years, it will be a more anticipated part of your Thanksgiving gathering than the pumpkin pie!

The process is simple: invite whomever you are spending Thanksgiving with to make an entry in your gratitude journal about the things for which they are thankful. They can write one or two sentences, create a short list, or compose an entire page or more in essay form. Each journal entry is then stored in a special Thanksgiving album, along with a few photographs and notes from that year's celebration.

For the first few years of our journal, there were several family members (namely my father and brothers) who, not surprisingly, resisted writing a journal entry. I had to follow them around with pen in hand and be quite persistent in my pleading. Now, however, these same reluctant few immediately ask to see "that

"The Julian Family Thanksgiving Book" by Stacy Julian

Album: 8.5" x 11" three-ring binder, Stampin' Up

Rubber Stamps (wheat, scarecrow, corn, hay): Close To My Heart

Scissors: Deckle edge, Family Treasures

Sticker Letters (1995): Pebbles in My Pocket

Patterned Paper: 1993 page, The Paper Patch; 1995 page, Close to My Heart (additional lines drawn using colored markers)

Autumn Stationery (1993): Source unknown

Computer Font (title page): Source unknown

Other: Autumn border "squares" on 1995 spread were cut from a piece of stationery (source unknown).

Ideas to Note: The title page background was created by color copying a section of a tablecloth. The picture in the album cover frame is a print of a Norman Rockwell painting.

We have health and family... not much else matters Nov. 25, 1993

Walter Clark the original meets Walter Clark the sequel.

Doris, Walt, Barry, JoAnn, Dennis, Geof. Clark eating Thanksgiving dinner from Furr's cafeteria.

Thanksgiving book" upon arrival. They eagerly review their past entries and add a new one without any prodding. Our book is nearly a decade old and has already become a wonderful history for our extended families and close friends, as each person touches upon the year's major events and milestones and lends their unique perspective to the change and growth that has occurred.

THANKSGIVING GRATITUDE JOURNAL GUIDELINES

To get started with a Thanksgiving gratitude journal, create a title page for the entire book (a three-ring binder works best for this project). Include your family's name, a title and the date you started your journal.

FUN IDEA For the background of my title page, I made a color copy of a tablecloth that we traditionally use around Thanksgiving.

Next, create a simple journal page for your guests to write their entries on. You only need to make one "master" page, which you can then print or photocopy as needed each year to keep a supply on hand. My page (created on the computer) has a simple repetitive design and the words "Give Thanks" as a border along the bottom. Blank pages would also work just fine.

Invite each person at your Thanksgiving celebration to write an entry about the things they are grateful for

Our book *is nearly*

a decade old and has already

become a wonderful history

for our extended families

and close friends.

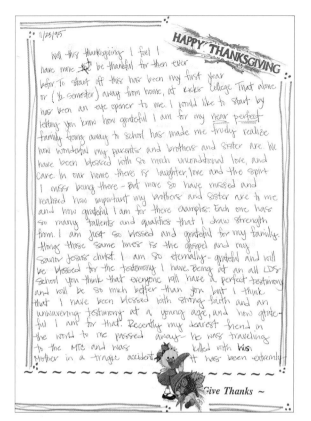

that year—and don't forget to create an entry yourself! (Some people might choose not to participate, and that's okay.) Remind everyone to date and sign their entries. You also might want to provide a permanent pen. If an entry doesn't fill up an entire page, simply have the next person continue on the same page, and encourage the writer to use only one side of the paper. If you'd like to facilitate the entries, consider giving one or two specific questions to respond to, such as:

- Who is someone you are grateful for and why?
- What one event this past year has brought you the most joy?
- Write about a personal triumph you experienced this year.
- What challenge or obstacle this year has taught you the most? What have you learned?
- List ten simple pleasures in your life that bring you happiness. Be specific.

You could even give everyone the same question and then enjoy reading all the different responses. The important thing is to capture what is in the hearts of those you choose to spend this great holiday with. I love looking back and enjoying the personality of each entry, evident through the personal handwriting and style of presentation, as well as the written words.

Finally, sometime after Thanksgiving Day, create a subtitle page or spread which will be placed in the album

PREPARATION

1. Purchase an 8.5" x 11" three-ring binder. Avoiding specialty albums (like spiral-bound albums) for this project is a good idea because of the many inserts and additions you'll be making over the years.

2. Purchase patterned paper and other decorative items with a fall or Thanksgiving theme.

3. Prepare a master journal entry page (see Guidelines, facing page, for more info).

4. Make sure you have several permanent-ink pens on hand for writing journal entries.

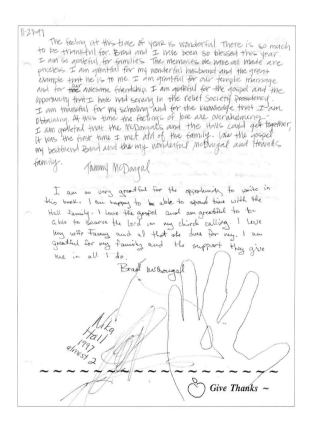

at the beginning of that year's journal entries. Include the year, a few photographs, and journaling describing anything significant about that year's celebration. Add a few decorative enhancements to finish off the page.

Here are a few other ideas for your subtitle page:

• Take a group photograph, along with several candid shots of those in attendance. Thanksgiving is also often a good time to capture multiple generations on film—always take advantage of such opportunities!

• You might include fun memorabilia items related to that year, such as a greeting card, special recipe, movie tickets from one of the new releases that weekend or a copy of the newspaper sports section listing the big football games. In 1995, I added a humorous little shopping list my dad sent me as a fun "thank you" (with a check!) for providing dinner for two of my college-age siblings.

• Capture anything unusual or unique about that year's festivities. For example, in 1997 my entire family participated in the "Cold Turkey RRRun." In remembrance of the freezing conditions we suffered, I made a color copy of the T-shirt we received and used it for my subtitle page decoration instead of traditional fall embellishments.

• Finish off each year's section by adding a closing border that coordinates with the design of the subtitle page. I often add a strip of patterned paper or a few coordinating embellishments on the bottom of the last journal page for that year.

FUN IDEA

If you're invited to spend the holiday with friends, don't forget your journal! I simply ask our hosts if, in addition to my corn casserole, I can bring my Thanksgiving Book. It has always been a welcome and positive part of our gatherings.

Lincoln stated in his Proclamation of Thanksgiving: "It has seemed to me fit and proper that they [the gracious gifts of the Most High God] should be solemnly, reverently and gratefully acknowledged as with one heart and one voice by the whole American People." Start today with your own proclamation to record and acknowledge the things you, your family and your special friends are thankful for with "one heart and one voice" in a special Thanksgiving journal.

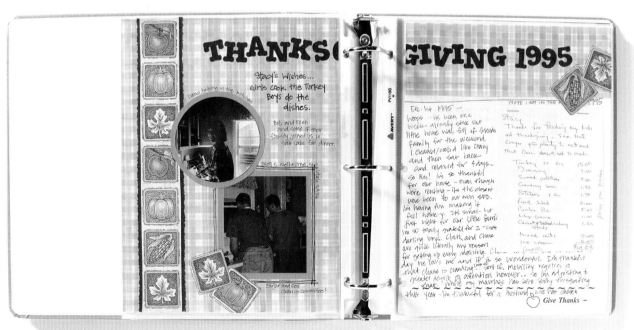

I'M PRETTY LOUSY AT KEEPING IN TOUCH WITH friends and family, which is probably why I love Christmas cards, letters, and photos so much. At least once a year, I can count on getting some "old-fashioned" mail. You know, the kind you have to go outside to the mailbox for, the kind that comes with a pretty postage stamp, the kind that can be savored and read over and over again. I love ignoring my mile-long holiday to-do list for a few moments while I sit and read a Christmas card and a newsy family letter. I feel like I've welcomed a much-anticipated guest—without even having to clean my house!

After reading each card, I display it prominently alongside others throughout my home until it's time to take the decorations down. What then? Since I can't bring myself to throw the cards and photos away (seems like an awfully unfriendly thing to do), I just pack them away in a box somewhere, never to be enjoyed again. Until last year, that is! I now have a "Christmas Letters and Photos" scrapbook to store the photos and favorite cards we receive, along with our own yearly photo and family letter. I even added sections for collecting holiday postage stamps and preserving letters to Santa Claus. This is one of the easiest projects in this book, cute enough to display and very useful at the same time!

"Christmas Letters and Photos" by Stacy Julian

Album: 8.5" x 11" Holiday Memories, Frances Meyer

Patterned Paper: Plaid and holly leaf, Frances Meyer; Lavender weave, Northern Spy

Snowman Mailing Label (used for photo mats): Frances Meyer

Sticker Letters (Favorite Cards page): Déjà Views, C-Thru Ruler Co.

Letter and Number Stencil: ABC Tracer, EK Success

Snowflake Punch: Emaginations

Mailbox Stationery (Letters to Santa page): Frances Meyer

White Embossed Paper (title page): Lasting Impressions

Mylar Self-adhesive Photo Sleeves: The C.R. Gibson Company

Paper in Snowman Scarf: Colors by Design

Black Velveteen Paper (snowman's hat): Paper Adventures

Ideas to Note: To soften the overall subtitle page and maintain the feel of snow, a sheet of vellum was placed over the patterned paper and several ripped paper edges were used.

After reading each card,

I display *it prominently*

alongside others throughout

my home until it's time

to take the decorations down.

What then?

FUN IDEA

CHRISTMAS CARDS AND PHOTOS BOOK GUIDELINES

Select a decorative theme for your album (see "Preparation") and you're ready to start creating your title page! Include your family's name and the date you began your album. Since my album features snowmen, I made a paper-pieced snowman and included the subtitle "Hearing from Friends is Snow Much Fun."

Next, create a subtitle page for each yearly section in your album, following the same format for each. Since the purpose of these pages is to introduce that year's cards and photos, make the year a prominent part of the page design. I had fun giving the years in my book a "snow-capped" look by sponging white ink along the top edge of the paper before cutting out the stenciled numbers (or letters). Then, include one or two holiday photographs and coordinating page decorations to go along with your album's theme. The photos don't necessarily have to coincide with the year featured on that page. For example, I found several snowman photos from years past to use throughout my book. I also added a fun snowman quote and portion of a holiday carol. You can make several subtitle pages at once for the next few years, so updating your album is quick and easy.

If you've been saving your old Christmas cards and letters, create a special "Christmas Past" section at the beginning of your album, rather than adding sections for each previous year. Sort through

your saved items, pull out your favorites and display them in your book!

Then, within each year's section, add the following three "fill-in" pages.

FAMILY PHOTO AND LETTER. If you write a family newsletter each year, include a copy in your album, along with a family photo from that year. (If you don't write a letter, simply mount a family photo on a page and add a few decorations.) I also like to keep a copy of the Christmas card we sent out that year, so I attach a small Mylar photo pocket to the outside of the page protector holding our family newsletter. I place the card and our photo in the photo pocket. This way, the card can easily be removed, allowing the letter to be read at the same time without removing it from the protector. (I insert our letter back-to-back with the subtitle page.) By keeping your own family's letters and photos, you'll have a mini family history highlighting the major events of each year!

PHOTO POCKET. To effortlessly store the photos you receive from family and friends, insert two sheets of patterned paper back-to-back in a page protector. Then, simply slide photos in on both sides of this quick "pocket page"—no need to mount them individually. Photos can be easily removed and enjoyed and yet take up very little space in the album. Make sure that each photo is labeled and has the year written on it somewhere, so it can be re-filed correctly if it's separated from the album.

FAVORITE CARDS PAGE. After Christmas is over, select a few of your favorite cards to keep in your book. I have each family member pick his or her favorite card. Choose one card to mount on a piece of patterned paper, then add the year and a "Favorite Cards" title. (I also include a photo of the sender if it fits on the page.) Slide your other favorite cards behind the patterned sheet in the same page protector.

As much as I'd like to save all the letters and cards we receive, I know this just isn't realistic. The photos are my "must save," and our selection of a few favorite cards each year will grow into a wonderful collection capturing the style and history of holiday greeting cards—something I love. I decided against saving the newsletters, since I knew I realistically would probably never go back and read them again. However, if you like to save the newsletters you receive, by all means do! (And see the variation section below for an idea on preserving them.)

At the end of your album, you might enjoy adding these optional sections:

LETTERS TO SANTA. This is the perfect home for copies of letters that your children pen to Mr. Claus. What fun to preserve their "wish lists" for future generations! (Make sure that the year is noted somewhere on the letter.) We have even received several responses from Santa at our house, and these are also stored in this section.

HOLIDAY STAMP COLLECTION. I think it's fun to collect the special postage stamps issued each year for holiday greetings. I simply adhere them to a piece of cardstock, creating a quick stamp collage. Each stamp already has the year right on it, so no further labeling is required. We even have a few extra-special stamps from foreign countries. It will be fun to watch our collage grow!

1   Choose a holiday-related theme and color scheme for your album. For example, my album uses a snowman theme, with lavender, plaid, and holly accents.

2   Select and purchase a three-ring binder. You can find many special holiday albums (like mine) that have coordinating supplies readily available.

3   Purchase several coordinating sheets of patterned paper and other holiday decorative elements, such as stationery, stickers, or punches. Often, you can find a line of mix-and-match holiday supplies made by the same company. If you can, stock up on your supplies and keep them in a special file for future yearly updates.

BECKY HIGGINS HAS A FUN VARIATION IDEA FOR storing your Christmas cards, photos and letters. Becky creates a two-page "pocket spread" to hold the cards and photos she receives. Since the actual cards aren't as important to Becky as the personalized messages, she cuts out the written notes to save in her scrapbook so the album doesn't become too bulky. Then, she stacks the newsletters she receives in page protectors (panoramic sheet protectors work well), keeping them unfolded and easily enjoyed!

Becky decorates the front of her pockets with postage stamps and address labels cut out from the cards and letters received that year. She keeps her Christmas pocket pages in her regular chronological album, but you could also put them in a separate holiday album.

When next Christmas has come and gone, you won't have to wonder what to do with all those cards, letters, and photos. You'll have a special place where you can preserve and enjoy your Christmas mail year round!

Now you'll have a **special** *place where you can* **preserve** *and* enjoy *your Christmas mail year round.*

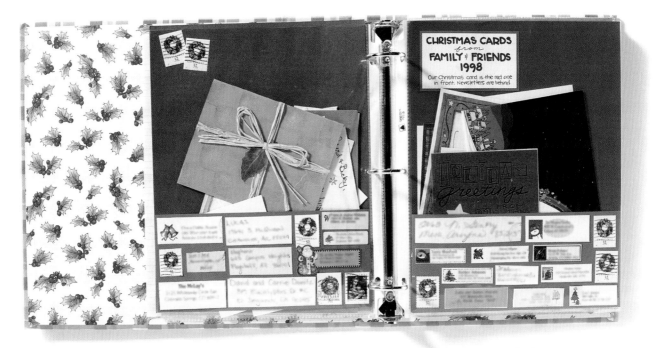

"Christmas Pocket Spread" by Becky Higgins

Dual Tone Paper: Paper Adventures

Patterned Paper (plaid background): Scrapbook Adventures

Christmas Exchange Album

Let's face it—even with all its merry festivities, Christmastime can add some stress to your life. So many things to do, places to go, presents to buy. There's often a dilemma of wanting to give meaningful gifts to all of your loved ones but being limited by a tight budget. Several years ago, my siblings and I faced this quandary. We wanted to exchange gifts between our respective families, but since most of us were still in school we simply couldn't afford it. We weren't fond of drawing names, because we wanted to remember each person every year.

Our solution? The Hall Cousins' Christmas Exchange Album! Just like it sounds, this fun album centers around an exchange of family scrapbook layouts. Toward the end of the year, each family creates a two-page layout summarizing life in their home during the past year. Then, we simply make enough color copies for each family, keeping the originals for ourselves. Each of us has a matching binder (thanks to

"The Hall Cousins' Christmas Exchange Album" by Stacy Julian

TITLE PAGE

Patterned Paper: Green checks, dots and plaid, Paper Patch; Red border and present, Colors by Design

Small Present: O Scrap, Imaginations, Inc.

Bows on Gifts: Kangaroo & Joey

Letter Stencil: Provo Craft

1998 SUBTITLE PAGE

Computer Font: DJ Crayon, DJ Inkers

1999 SUBTITLE PAGE

Stocking Patterned Paper: Frances Meyer

Large Stocking Die Cut and Bell Stickers: Frances Meyer

Plaid Patterned Paper: Close To My Heart

My favorite part

of the whole project

is being able to

preserve *the unique*

perspective *that each*

sibling *shares.*

Mom and Dad) for storing our collection of pages.

Christmas 2000 will mark the fifth anniversary of our exchange album and while most of us would now be able to give more expensive gifts, we all agree that nothing else could equal the value of the family record we're compiling. I anticipate receiving each family's layout as much or more than any other gift under the tree. My favorite part of the whole project is being able to preserve the unique perspective that each sibling shares through these pages. While I can create a layout featuring photos of my extended family, it's presented from my point of view. To have a collection of pages capturing each person's personality and perspectives is priceless! As much as we cherish our relationships with extended family, they are among the easiest aspects of our lives to leave out of our scrapbooks. This is a great project for putting them back in!

CHRISTMAS EXCHANGE ALBUM GUIDELINES

There's very little work required to start your album, since most of the pages will come from someone else. All you need are a title page and subtitle pages to divide your album into sections.

On the title page, include a name for your album and the date it was started. I added the saying, "Family . . . the true gift of Christmas." Then have fun decorating it with some holiday-related embellishments.

If you're just starting an exchange album, you can help get everyone excited by creating identical title pages for each family album (or title pages personalized with each family's name). Next, decide how you want to organize your album. I've divided mine into yearly sections containing all the pages I receive each particular year. You could also divide your album into family sections, storing all the pages received from each individual family chronologically within each section. Either way, create a subtitle page, containing either the year or the family name, for each section. While each subtitle page doesn't have to look exactly the same, try to use a similar layout design. For example, I used a piece of holiday

patterned paper as the background, with a square in the center containing the year and a few larger decorations inspired from the patterned paper. Adding tabs to the page protectors holding your subtitle pages makes it easier to look through your album later.

Now all that's left is to create your own family's two-page spread for the year! Try to make each year's layout different from the previous year's. You don't even need to use holiday decorations (most of the time we don't). Simply select a handful of photographs that summarize your family's experiences and activities that year, then arrange them on the pages and add some journaling and a few decorations.

Selecting which photos to use is probably the hardest part of this project. Think about these possibilities:
- Major events like births, graduations and weddings.
- Everyday things like a photo of Dad or Mom at work, children playing together or showing off one of their school projects.
- Activities you enjoy doing together, like biking or bowling.
- Family vacations, moves or major purchases (like a trampoline or new car).
- A family member's goal or personal achievement. For example, last year my brother decided to work really hard and enter a body-building contest. I love the fact that my sister-in-law included a photograph

1   Commit each person in your extended family group to participate. Involve as many family members as you want!

2   Choose a style and size of album that will work for everyone. We each have an 8.5" x 11" three-ring binder. If needed, purchase an album to store your collection in.

3   Try to file photographs away throughout the year that you think might work for your family's page. This will save precious time during a busy season.

4   Purchase a selection of holiday-themed patterned papers and decorative elements for your title and subtitle pages. If there are members of the group that don't scrapbook, make sure they know where to get archival supplies.

5   Set a time or deadline for the exchange. We generally send our pages through the mail, but if you are all able to gather at a family party, you could exchange your pages in person.

of his fine-tuned muscles on their layout. (He won third place too!)

Involve your entire family in the selection process—perhaps have each person choose one or two photos they feel are most important. Keep in mind that more is not always better. While a collage of several photographs can be a great way to go, you might choose one year to include only an updated family portrait and then list a few major events from each month. After you've created your family's spread, have the appropriate number of color copies made.

FUN IDEA

When making color copies, use a 5% reduction (95% of original) to make sure you don't lose any information close to the edges. Mail (or hand-deliver) your copies and file the originals in your own binder. Then sit back and wait for the other layouts to arrive!

An exchange album doesn't have to revolve around Christmas—and it doesn't even have to involve your family! Why not plan an annual page exchange during the summer? Or start one as a way to stay in touch with college friends or a group of former neighbors.

I love what this one simple project has brought to my extended family. It's been one small way to de-commercialize Christmas and return to the central theme of love and giving of self. Instead of scouring the stores for that "just right" candle, book, frame, calendar or CD for my brothers and sisters, I can spend that time creating something very meaningful that each will keep and treasure in their home. After all, it's when we give of ourselves that we truly give!

Great Resources for Simple Scrapbooks

Wondering where you can find some of the products used in the scrapbooks throughout this book? It's impossible to provide a complete list of product suppliers—there are hundreds of retail and online stores that sell quality scrapbook supplies. Instead, I've tried to put together resource information on a few product suppliers to perhaps help you get started or track down a specific product you've seen here.

ALBUMS

CENTURY PHOTO PRODUCTS AND ACCESSORIES
(800) 767-0777 or www.centuryphoto.com.
Call for a mail-order catalog. Album selection varies with each catalog. In addition to albums, they offer a variety of regular and divided page protectors.

CLOSE TO MY HEART
Sold through independent consultants, call (888) 655-6552 to find one near you or go to www.dotadventures.com. Post-bound albums in 12" x 12" and 6" x 6" sizes.

DALEE BOOK CO.
(800) 852-2665 or www.daleebook.com. Available at scrapbook stores everywhere. Post-bound albums with fabric and leather covers, available in 12" x 12", 8.5" x 11" and 6" x 8" sizes.

FRANCES MEYER
(800) 372-6237 or www.francesmeyer.com.
Available at scrapbook stores everywhere. Three-ring binders that coordinate with patterned paper, available in 12" x 12" and 8.5" x 11" sizes.

GENERATIONS BY HAZEL
(314) 542-5400 or www.generationsbyhazel.com. Sold through specialty stores. Post-bound albums (12" x 12", 8.5" x 11" and 5" x 7") and three-ring binders (12" x 12" and 8.5" x 11") in a variety of cover styles.

HILLER BOOK AND BINDERS
(801) 521-2411, www.hillerindustries.com or ask your local scrapbook store. Three-ring albums in 12" x 12", 8.5" x 11" and 5.5" x 8.5" sizes, with a variety of cover styles, including tapestry covers. Spiral-bound albums also available.

KOLO
(860) 547-0367 or www.kolo-usa.com. Available at book and craft stores. Post-bound albums with a cut-out cover window in a variety of sizes from 5.5" x 7.5" to 12" x 13".

SEW BE IT, TIMELESS TAPESTRY PHOTO ALBUMS
(801) 299-9019 or www.timelesstapestry.com.
Three-ring and post-bound albums in 5.5" x 8.5", 8.5" x 11" and 12" x 12" sizes, a large selection of tapestry and fabric covers.

STAMPIN' UP!
(800) Stamp Up or www.stampinup.com to find a demonstrator near you. Three-ring 8.5" x 11" albums that can be personalized with a cover photo, threaded ribbon and rubber stamps. They also offer 12" x 12" post-bound albums and a variety of divided page protectors.

PAPERS & DECORATIVE ELEMENTS

CLOSE TO MY HEART
(888) 655-6552 or www.dotadventures.com to contact a consultant close to you. Full line of rubber stamp and scrapbook supplies, including 60+ colors of cardstock and coordinating patterned paper.

FRANCES MEYER
(800) 372-6237 or www.francesmeyer.com. Large selection of themed papers, frames, stickers and other scrapbook supplies.

K & COMPANY
(888) 244-2083 or www.kandcompany.com.
Embossed papers, frames and decorative items.

KEEPING MEMORIES ALIVE
(800) 419-4949 or www.scrapbooks.com. Full line of supplies, including Fabric Brites line of coordinating paper.

LASTING IMPRESSIONS FOR PAPER, INC.
(801) 298-1983 or check your local specialty store.
Embossed papers and coordinating patterns.

MY MIND'S EYE
(801) 298-3709 or www.frame-ups.com. Available at scrapbook stores everywhere. Punch-out kids, frames, titles and journaling blocks that coordinate together.

PROVO CRAFT
(801) 377-4311 or www.provocraft.com. Available at scrapbook stores everywhere. Computer fonts, coordinating watercolor papers, sticker letters and much more.

STICKER PLANET (SUZY'S ZOO AND MORE)
(800) 557-8678 or www.stickerplanet.com.
Complete sticker lines in all kinds of styles.

Index

Other Titles from
Creating Keepsakes Books

www.creatingkeepsakes.com

THE ART OF CREATIVE LETTERING: 50 AMAZING NEW ALPHABETS YOU CAN MAKE FOR SCRAPBOOKS, CARDS, INVITATIONS, AND SIGNS by Becky Higgins with Siobhán McGowan. Easy instructions for making creative alphabets, with lots of scrapbook-page samples for inspiration. Paperback $19.95, ISBN 1-929180-11-x. Hardcover $25.00, ISBN 1-929180-10-1.

BABY ALPHABETS CD by Becky Higgins. An easy-to-use CD of fonts for all kinds of fun projects including 15 fonts from Becky's book *The Art of Creative Lettering*. $14.95, ISBN 1-929180-26-8.

MOM'S LITTLE BOOK OF DISPLAYING CHILDREN'S ART by Lisa Bearnson with Julie Taboh. Seventy-five ideas for creatively displaying your children's creations. Hardcover $16.95, ISBN 1-929180-16-0.

MOM'S LITTLE BOOK OF PHOTO TIPS by Lisa Bearnson and Siobhán McGowan. A mom-to-mom advice book that's completely nontechnical and emphasizes the creative side of photography. Hardcover $16.95, ISBN 1-929180-12-8.

WEDDING ALPHABET CD by Becky Higgins. Fifteen elegant fonts for all occasions from Becky's book *The Art of Creative Lettering*. $14.95, ISBN 1-929180-25-x.

WEDDING KEEPSAKES: HUNDREDS OF BEAUTIFUL, EASY IDEAS FOR INVITATIONS, PROGRAMS, AND SCRAPBOOKS YOU CAN MAKE FOR YOUR WEDDING by Siobhán McGowan. For the bride-to-be, projects and ideas from invitations to thank-you notes to scrapbook pages. Paperback $19.95, ISBN 1-929180-18-7. Hardcover $25.00, ISBN 1-929180-17-9.